Unleashing Your Creativity on a Shoestring

Breaking new ground . . .
without breaking the bank

Janice Armstrong

A & C I

First published in Great Britain 2008

A & C Black Publishers Ltd
38 Soho Square, London W1D 3HB
www.acblack.com

No responsibility for loss caused to any individual or organisation acting or refraining from action as a result of the
material in this publication can be accepted by A & C Black
Publishers Ltd or the author.

A CIP record for this book is available from the British Library.

ISBN: 9-780-7136-7544-3

This book is produced using paper that is made from wood grown in
managed, sustainable forests. It is natural, renewable and recyclable.
The logging and manufacturing processes conform to the environ-
mental regulations of the country of origin.

Design by Fiona Pike, Pike Design, Winchester
Typeset by RefineCatch, Bungay, Suffolk
Printed in the Spain by Graphycems

CONTENTS

ACKNOWLEDGEMENTS

This book is dedicated to the memory of my mum and dad who taught me the joy of creativity from an early age through cooking, gardening and music.

Many of the clients and colleagues I have worked with have provided me with ideas and inspiration for this book. Thank you all.

A huge thank you to Lisa Carden at A&C Black for her patience, understanding, support and advice. I couldn't have done it without you.

A special thanks to my friend and colleague Hannah Nutley for her encouragement and advice and for being a great coach.

Thanks to my sisters Valda and Adele, whom I adore. I am so lucky to have such a wonderful family.

Finally to Neil, my soul mate – thank you, thank you, thank you for everything, but in particular for constantly broadening my horizons with fresh experiences and for making me laugh out loud; and our wonderful, beautiful daughter Evie, who never fails to amaze and inspire me and who stretches my creative talents every day.

1 INTRODUCTION

When I set out to write this book it was with one purpose: to encourage everyone to realise that they have more ideas than they could ever imagine. I wanted to write a simple guide that you could dip into any time to find inspiration and fresh ways of thinking.

Our inner demons taunt us with the idea that we're not creative enough – that creativity is something special that a select few are born with. In my experience, we are all far more creative than we give ourselves credit for and I hope that by the end of this book you too will be convinced.

If you run your own business or manage a team, you know instinctively the importance of creativity. But how to bring it to life and make it 'real' is often a harder proposition. As well as equipping you with the tools to be creative, this book contains tips on how to lead a creative movement in your business and really make it stick. After all, creativity is only worth its salt if you do something with it. There's no point in having lots of ideas that don't go anywhere or that don't – crucially – improve your bottom line. This book is about creativity with a purpose – everyday creativity that you can action all the time in order to come up with bigger and better ideas to solve the challenges you face.

While organisations of all sizes will benefit from an injection of new thinking, creativity is especially vital for small businesses. When there are fewer people doing a wide range of tasks, you've got to be able to think laterally and make the most of your lean structure and quick decision-making. According to the Federation of Small Businesses (FSB), *90% of innovation in the UK comes from small businesses.* That's an exciting thought. When you consider the big successes of recent years, the story of a couple of people working away in the spare room or round the kitchen table is now a familiar one. Take companies as diverse as Google, eBay, Dyson, Bravissimo, Rachel's Organic or even Friends Reunited: all involve one or two individuals who had a fantastic idea and then used it to power them to business growth and success.

All innovation starts with an idea and this book is all about coming up with ideas and then putting them into action. Everyone has the ability to do it, but you have to have the right attitude: if you think you can't do it, you'll never reach your full potential. The fastest route to creativity is to do something you wouldn't normally do. Setting time aside to let freshness in will change your life – and not just your life at work. There are challenges at the beginning of each chapter aimed at getting you to think and behave in a different way, to open the window and set your creativity free.

Challenge: What is your favourite habit? Something you always do and love doing? Now break the habit and do something different. It will shake you out of your usual pattern. The lack of something that is so familiar to you will awaken you to new thoughts, possibilities and experiences.

What is creativity?

The poet A E Housman said 'I could no more define poetry than a terrier can define a rat, but that I thought we both recognized the object by the symptoms which it provokes in us.'

Creativity feels like a pretty elusive thing. Clichéd phrases like 'blue sky thinking' and 'thinking outside the box' spring to mind, but for me, they don't help much. I work at Clear, a company that helps businesses come up with big ideas to grow their brands, products and people. My job is to train teams to come up with their own ideas, and provide them with the skills to bring these ideas to life within their organisations.

I decided to ask around to see if I could get closer to a more meaningful answer to the big question – what on earth is creativity? When I asked my colleagues for their thoughts, thankfully it all started to feel more tangible:

- 'It's a new and different way of solving an old problem.'
- 'It's about a sense of curiosity that leads to the discovery of a solution.'
- 'It's the simple ability to see a different or better way of doing something.'

One definition from the 20th-century American advertising guru James Webb Young explains it brilliantly: 'Creativity is nothing more nor less than a new combination of old elements.' What I like about this is it makes it sound so easy. And it is! It demystifies all that can get in the way between us and an idea – which is what creativity is about.

For me, creativity is as much about how you behave as what you do. It's about taking small steps to create a big difference. It's about building momentum within yourself and the people you work with. It's also contagious. When you start working and thinking more creatively, it will encourage other people to do the same. People will relax, feel energised and less constrained. You'll start to enjoy meetings (yes, really). Ideas will come much more easily and you'll start making connections. Creativity is what keeps small businesses and their people thriving. It's exciting stuff!

The power of creativity

Have you ever been in a meeting or out with friends when

you've had a light bulb moment and thought 'that's a great idea!'? Chances are that if you sat down and analysed it, it will have been something very simple and obvious: the best ideas usually are. Every day we come up with good ideas – ways to solve a tricky situation at work, techniques for keeping the peace at home with our children. We are constantly inventing, learning, circumventing difficulties – all creative behaviours that we seldom give ourselves credit for. If you believe Andy Law, who set up the ad agency St Luke's, creativity is also extremely powerful: 'Creativity can provide all the solutions to the complex problems of the workplace. Creative thinking is a positive, generative force that uses imagination to power business.'

Natalie Turner runs her own small business helping companies with innovation and managing change. 'When you're with a client, you've got to be able to think on your feet and make connections,' she says. 'You've got to be agile and responsive to their changing needs. The ability to think creatively is essential in a small business, far more so than for larger companies.'

That said, businesses small and large are increasingly seeing the value of innovation. More and more of us are spending our office hours in innovative pursuits and according to the Department for Business, Enterprise and Regulatory Reform, 48% of firms now have employees involved in innovation – that's up from 32% in 2006.

New product ideas like the iPod are exciting and really capture people's imagination. But just as important are ideas to improve internal processes, company policy, customer satisfaction levels and so on. These won't attract the same headlines but they are all areas where creative thinking can make an enormous difference to your business. For example, why not encourage your team to start the day with a five-minute meeting? It will mean that everyone knows what their colleagues are doing and gives them a chance to add their suggestions to the melting pot too. It's a powerful way to build morale and improve the sharing of experience within the business.

In a former life, I was a BBC journalist and there, each day would begin with an 'ideas meeting'. Reporters and producers gathered to decide what stories were to be reported on that day and more importantly, *how* those stories were to be covered. If you've run the same story every day for a week – the war in Iraq, for example – *how* you cover the story is crucial. You're looking for new angles to keep the story fresh: the implications politically in the UK and elsewhere in the world, for soldiers, civilians and for their families.

The reason that particular ideas meeting existed was to set the news agenda for what viewers would be watching that evening. And the plan was to give them a range of stories: a mixture of light and shade. Every story every day required fresh thinking, a new approach, creative ideas. What I discovered was that journalism and creativity have a common bond; both require a curiosity about the world. 'I wonder why he said that?', 'What if we did it another way?', 'What makes you think that will happen?'

It's very easy to take what we see at face value, to take life and experiences for granted, to assume we know the answer or risk losing face by admitting we don't. After an interview with a newly appointed education minister who had been promoted rapidly through the ranks, I asked him why he thought he had got the job. He replied that he wasn't afraid to ask naive questions. Whatever job he was in, he would look around and ask the obvious in order to understand fully what was going on. 'Why do we do that?' and 'What's it for?'

Coming to a new job gives you a great opportunity to see the situation with fresh eyes. Once you've been there for a while, you become acclimatised to your new surroundings and stop seeing so clearly. The education minister said he always wrote down his initial thoughts so that he could remember what something was first like and what his impressions were. I've since discovered some of the people who are best in their field, whatever their line of work, are those who aren't afraid to ask the seemingly 'stupid' questions – the ones that appear glaringly obvious, but that often elicit the most interesting answers.

When you run your own business, obviously you're not starting a new job, but it's important regularly to step outside your familiar routine in order to see things differently. Ask new joiners for their honest first impressions, and don't hold what they say against them! Don't get defensive or take things personally: you have invested a lot (in every sense) in your business, but companies of all sizes can benefit from a wake-up call. Take advantage of this useful information, treasure it and respond accordingly.

So the importance of asking questions, from both inside and outside the business, is clearly apparent. The most appropriate ones for your company will, of course, depend on what industry it operates in and what challenges it's currently facing, but they could be:

■ What would happen if we didn't work 9 to 5?
■ Does our production line work in the most efficient way possible?

- If we switched suppliers, what would be the impact?
- How would we cope if a new shop offering the same type of products opened in the next town?

In meetings, listen to your 'inner voice' as to well as to what you are actually hearing. At times, I have written down what's been said on the right page of my notebook and noted down on the opposite page my personal response to the conversation. It's often the case that the left-hand page is the more interesting and can spark creative thoughts.

Like learning to ride a bike, creativity needs practice for you to get the hang of it. If you don't ride a bike for years, you'll probably be a bit wobbly when you next have another go until you regain your confidence. Creativity is no different: we have no problems with it when we're younger, but at some stage many of us simply get out of the habit of being creative.

One of the myths about creativity is that it's a bit 'wacky' and for slightly weird, hippy types. Sadly, I don't feel that describes me or most of my colleagues. It might make for an even more colourful office if it were true!

The perspiration/inspiration balance

To paraphrase Thomas Edison's famous saying, having ideas is as much about work and effort as being wacky and creative.

Generating ideas is part of a process and you need to allow time to explore them. Sit with them, familiarise yourself with them, reflect on them. Once you've done this, you can embark on them . . . but don't rush this bit. Get others involved. Sound people out and listen to what they say. A word of caution here, however. Choose carefully the people you want to involve in this. There will always be some who will shoot down your ideas all too quickly. That's not to say you shouldn't listen to criticism — some of it can be incredibly useful — but just be aware that ideas are fragile and many never progress if they're shared in the wrong way or with the wrong people. Think of those who are a positive force in your life and work and ask them for their input.

In the early stages of creativity, there is no right or wrong: there are only alternatives. And for ideas to flourish we need to find a way of suspending judgement. I know how hard it can be to do this, and when I'm running workshops on creativity, I can see people struggling with it. More often than not, our first impulse is to give our reaction to an idea, and it's usually a criticism or a reason why it might not work or be the best idea. In the analytical world, this is how we work. Don't despair if you recognise yourself here, you're not alone.

When Art Fry came up with the idea of the Post-it™ Note it was turned down by his bosses. Fry sang in a choir and became frustrated that the little scraps of paper he had in his hymn book were constantly falling out. He remembered that he had previously come up with a glue that would stick things down but that would come off just as easily. It had been shelved because it didn't work. He went back to work, found the glue and reformulated it. He then applied it to paper and cut it into blocks. When his idea was met with a lukewarm response, he supplied his little blocks to all the secretaries in the company. When they ran out, there was an outcry – he had hit upon a hitherto unknown need.

Although Post-its™ are just one of a staggering 55,000 products made by 3M, they're certainly one of the most famous, and Art Fry, who's now retired, still gives talks on the value of creativity in business.

At this stage then, no idea is a bad one. Making a decision too soon could mean you miss out on a profitable opportunity. What we need for now is to protect ideas because they are still just 'seedlings'. This process is called 'greenhousing' or 'hot-housing'. In the same way as you would look after a small plant, ideas need shelter, nourishment and care. They need to be kept in a safe place where they can take root and grow until they are ready to be harvested. It's not always obvious at the outset which ones are going to flourish – it takes time before you can judge their real significance – so you need to treat them all in the same way.

Writing down your problem or challenge is a great way to harness your creativity. In order to be creative, you need to feel safe and committing something to writing is a way of creating a safe space while you mull things over. It also gives you control over your problem. Start by finding a blank piece of paper and jotting down your challenge in the middle. Then around it, write down all the possible solutions to your problem. This simple Mind Map™ (a concept invented by the author and psychologist Tony Buzan) allows you to see all your options and make connections between them, rather than leaving it as a massive problem spinning around in your head.

Let's say that your challenge is a common one for a small business owner: you feel as though you don't have enough time to tackle all the jobs you need to get through every day. Using the Mind Map, you could note down some of the potential solutions:

- just do less – accept compromise
- delegate
- try different ways to do the jobs
- ask for extensions on deadlines
- re-prioritise work

Look to see if there are any connections between your solutions or any way you can combine them to make even greater impact. Assess each one and note down the pros and cons before deciding on what action to take. Start by looking for the low hanging fruit – those solutions that are easiest to achieve and with the highest impact.

Go for the low hanging fruit

	Low impact	High impact
Difficult to do		Put plans in place
Easy to do	Background job	Action straight away

Lighting the spark

Being creative is about trying new things and having new experiences and thoughts. It's experiential and it's fun! Try doing something that you've never done before. Read a magazine you've never read, or take a different journey into work. It's about simple techniques that can and do lead to new outcomes.

Admitting you are creative can feel like a dangerous thing to do. According to Gordon MacKenzie in his book *Orbiting the Giant Hairball* (Viking, 1998), a first grade class at an American primary school was asked 'how many artists are there in the room?' En masse, the children leapt from their seats waving their arms. The same question was put to a class in second grade. This time, about half raised their hands, shoulder high – no higher. In third grade, at best 10 children out of 30 would raise a hand tentatively and self-consciously. By the time they reached sixth grade, no more than one or two children raised their hands and then only slightly, betraying a fear of being identified by the group as a 'closet artist'. MacKenzie's view on this is 'every school was participating in the suppression of creative genius'.

The author Jordan Ayan highlights a similar situation. He writes, 'My wife and I went to a kindergarten parent/teacher conference and were informed that our budding refrigerator artist, Christopher, would be receiving a grade of "unsatisfactory" in Art. We were shocked. How could any child — let alone our child — receive a poor grade in Art at such a young age? His teacher informed us that he had refused to color within the lines, which was a state requirement for demonstrating "grade-level motor skills".'

I feel sad about this. Somewhere along the line, we stop being creative or certainly stop thinking of ourselves as creative and start to doubt our abilities. It's not much wonder then that by the time we are let loose in the workplace we are convinced we've lost it altogether. That, combined with the pressures of the bottom line and making fast decisions, can easily extinguish any small spark of creativity.

Being honest, how do you fare in this? Are you encouraging or suppressing the creative genius inside yourself or your team? What's your immediate reaction when you hear an idea? 'Is this a good idea or bad?' 'Will it work?' 'Is it practical?' 'Are there any holes in the thinking?' If this is a familiar pattern, you are not alone. At school we are trained to look for right or wrong. We are marked highly when we get the answer right, penalised when we get it wrong. But this type of culture on its own is very damaging to the growth of new ideas. It's a sure-fire way to kill germinating seeds of inspiration and will soon deter any person who suggests them.

When we're busy at work or thinking about work, watching television or planning what to cook for dinner, there's precious little time for creativity. The brain is a pretty amazing piece of equipment, but it can only do so much at a time. When we're preoccupied, we're using up valuable brain space. When we relax, we free up some of this space for creativity. So sit back, relax, take a few deep breaths and make room for creativity.

2 WHAT SORT OF A PERSON ARE YOU?

Challenge: Buy yourself a journal – an attractive notebook – and use it to jot down your thoughts, feelings and doodles as you read this book. With a pencil in hand, note the answers to the questions in this chapter and pay attention to your reactions as you go through.

Before embarking on your creative journey, it's worth getting to know yourself a bit better. It's useful to put a stake in the ground so you understand where you are currently – the context in which you and the people working with you are operating, and the implications of that.

This chapter is designed to encourage you to think about the kind of person you are and where your strengths lie, and to focus your mind on areas that need some attention. It's a quick reality check. Of course, there's always the option of giving yourself a sabbatical, packing a suitcase and travelling the world to find the answers to these questions. But if you're running a small business, that probably isn't an option at the moment! Instead, find a comfy chair, make yourself a cup of tea and allow yourself to do a bit of soul searching.

The importance of knowing yourself

Understanding more about yourself will help give some context to what's going on in your organisation at the moment. This isn't something that works bottom up – without the leadership from you, creativity is unlikely to succeed. Recognising what your barriers might be will enable you to build a firm foundation for change – and I'm assuming that if you're reading this book, then you're looking for some sort of change. Change only happens once you're aware of the need for a shake-up, and people need to feel confident and secure to be able to do this. Once you have this awareness of the kind of person you are, then you can start to create your vision for the future – how you want it to be.

Who do you want to be? Are you organised and methodical? Are you always coming up with ideas? Are you spontaneous – do you go with the flow? Do you always start with the hardest task first? Are you a list-maker? Do you write things down and work your way through, prioritising the most important tasks?

Do you start each day with a 'to do' list? Are you a morning or an evening person? Do you find yourself absorbed in a task and then realise it's way past lunch time? Do you have a place where you can work better than any other? Is there a time of day when you are most productive? Do you have a creative space where you find that ideas flow much more easily?

It's worth spending time thinking about some of these questions before you can start developing the necessary habits of a creative person. There's nothing magical about creativity, though it can produce magical results. Anyone and everyone can be creative and with a bit of practice and a few tools, you can become great at it.

Take a moment to think about the kind of person you are and the kind of person you want to be. Think about how the statements opposite apply to you, and tick 'often', 'sometimes' or 'never' depending on which seems most appropriate.

The importance of knowing yourself

One of the advantages of getting older is that we know who we are. Gone are the old insecurities of youth and in their place is self-assurance, confidence, an understanding of who we are and our place in the world. That's how it is . . . isn't it?

Not always, and even if you've reached a ripe old stage of total self-assurance, this in itself could be causing you problems. There may be obstacles blocking the way between you and your creative self. Many people feel that the way we

	Often	Sometimes	Never
1 I have a favourite place that I go to get in the creative flow.			
2 I block out a chunk of time each day to be creative.			
3 I work in an inspiring environment.			
4 I feel I bring my whole self to work.			
5 I regularly go for a walk to mull over problems.			
6 I find sleeping on a problem helps me find a solution.			
7 I feel like I'm on a treadmill.			
8 I am scared of acting, drawing or singing.			
9 Wearing a suit makes me feel better.			
10 I know when I am most creative.			

Scoring

Statements 1–6
Score 2 points for every time you replied 'never'.   _____

Statements 1–10
Score 1 point for every time you replied 'sometimes'.   _____

Statements 7–10
Score 2 points for every time you replied 'often'.   _____

Total points scored

14 points and above
Your creativity could definitely do with a helping hand.

8–12 points
Pretty good, but there's still room for improvement.

8 points and under
You are a creative person who has already developed some great techniques. Your skills will increase even more if you follow some of the suggestions in this book.

are is the result of our upbringing, determined by our genes and social circumstances. Every experience we have in life shapes us in some way. Every conversation we have confirms our view of the world and what to expect from it. In my view, this is true, but only up to a point. I also know that it's possible to choose to change, at any stage in life.

The way you think about yourself is crucial here. It determines what you say, think and feel. If you think of yourself as happy and confident, you will be. And so will everyone else. The same is true at work. If you believe yourself to ooze creativity, then you will.

The expression 'give me the boy and I'll show you the man' (albeit with a gender change) hit home in a conversation I had with a friend recently. She told me her eight-year-old daughter had been given a certificate for swimming 100 metres. I was genuinely impressed and congratulated her and Polly. I remember being able to swim 25 metres when I was much older than Polly and I thought it was a huge achievement. My friend told me she thought Polly had only managed it because *she* (her mum) didn't think she would. I felt very sad. If her own mother didn't believe in her daughter at the age of eight, she was indeed going to face an uphill struggle and her self-image is going to need some serious nurturing to convince her she is capable of achieving great things. Self-belief is one of the most important things that parents can give to a child, but it's arguably also one of the hardest.

People perform better when they are believed in. If you're able to convince those around you that there's no limit to what they will achieve, you'll reap enormous rewards both for yourself and for them too.

Exercise

With a pen and paper, spend five minutes writing down the answer to the question below. Just write what first comes to mind. This is an exercise I call 'the dinner party test'. If you were at a dinner party and you left the table for a few minutes, what would your friends say about you? What would you like them to say about you? E.g. 'He's a great boss who always treats people well and fairly.' 'She's got it all – successful career, great family and manages to juggle it all effortlessly.' This is about your gut feelings, so don't agonise over what you write or censor it! Aim for about 8–10 sentences.

Who do I think I am?

Now, move into another room and read what you have written out loud. How does it sound? Are you proud of it? If not, why not?

> Decide now that you are going to focus on the positives. The rest is getting in your way and you can live without it.
>
> By the time you have finished this book, I want you to know that you are a creative genius. You have star quality and deserve only the very best!

Understanding the hurdles

'Life is either a daring adventure or nothing at all.'
Helen Keller

There are two main obstacles that can combine to block creativity. The first is your environment; the second is you. The good news is that neither is insurmountable.

Sometimes taking the first step towards a new creative behaviour is the hardest part and feels like an extra challenge in itself. Perhaps you find the process scary or that it conjures up memories of bad or embarrassing experiences in art or music lessons back at school. Or maybe you just don't know how to get the ball rolling. Whatever the reason, the only important thing to do is to make a start, whatever your concerns are. Doing is never half as bad as thinking, and the chances are you'll surprise yourself.

A few years ago, I took a course at a management training school. Before lunch on the second day, one of the tutors triumphantly appeared with a huge box of pens, paper, crayons, glitter and glue, and announced we were to find a partner and draw a picture of the organisation we worked for. My heart sank. Couldn't we just skip this and have lunch? It had been such a long time since I'd drawn anything, let alone 'an organisation'. My mind was racing – art had never been my strong point. Everyone would have to hold up their picture at the end of the exercise. It would obviously be humiliating. I had magnified the task out of all proportion.

This was clearly not in the spirit of things. As I sat on the floor staring at the blank sheet of paper, I would rather have done anything else in the world. Instead, I suppose I faced my demons. I talked with my partner and found out her feelings weren't dissimilar to my own. We talked a little about our respective organisations and started putting crayon to paper. To my amazement I found that I was actually enjoying it. It became easy to talk about difficulties and gaps when you could sketch it out as you went along.

Apart from the fact that doing the exercise was great fun, what we learnt from it was astonishing. When we talked the rest of the team through our pictures, it was one of the most insightful experiences I have ever had. The clarity over where the problems lay and what needed to be done was there in all its glittery glory.

A few years on with a toddler in tow, getting stuck in with crayons is a far less scary prospect. I spend many happy days painting at the kitchen table and rolling and cutting with soft clay. My point is that getting started is the hard bit and once you've overcome your inner angst, I know you'll enjoy the ride.

Your environment

As a business owner or manager, you'll be keen to minimise risk. In a profit-driven environment, there's little time for random experiential processes that may or may not yield a reward. Creativity thrives in an atmosphere that is free from pressure and targets. This is very different from the way most businesses operate, where staff work long hours – often under considerable pressure – to meet targets and tight deadlines. This is a real hurdle for many people. Even if you *are* creative, the environment is working against you.

When you live and work in surroundings that support who you are as a person, it increases creativity. It frees you up to concentrate on the work in hand. For example:

- When you climb a mountain and stand back to look at the view, how do you feel?
- When you're sitting on the beach looking out to the horizon with the waves lapping at your toes, what are your thoughts?

■ What does it feel like to kick leaves in the park on a cold, bright autumn day?

There are certain places that are intrinsically motivating. They feel inspirational and you genuinely feel stimulated when you're there. This isn't a conscious thing; it just happens. When I'm in a beautiful place I try to take a mental 'photo' so I can capture it when I'm back at my desk. I take long, slow breaths and try to take it all in. These places allow us really to focus and concentrate on what's important. They help us see situations from new perspectives, jolt us out of the ordinary and encourage us to follow new, more attractive paths. In what ways could you bring these inspiring environments to work? How can you recreate these moments in your workspace? Spend a few moments designing your ideal workspace. Get out the crayons if you want to!

What do you want to achieve?

A good rule of thumb is to start with the end in mind. When Tom Watson, the founder of IBM, was asked why he thought it was such a successful company, he said it was down to three things. The first was that he had a very clear image in his mind of what he wanted his company to look like. Then he asked himself what he would need to do in order to make this happen. And then from day one, he began to act in a focused way in order to achieve it.

Free flow

Creativity requires a leap of faith. You need energy and desire to make it happen.

If you have these, the rest will fall into place and you'll inspire both yourself and everyone in your team to stretch their boundaries and keep creating. Try asking yourself questions such as:

- What kind of person do you want to be?
- What kinds of things do you enjoy?
- What did you enjoy as a child?
- When have you felt really satisfied?
- What makes you happy?
- When you look back on your life, what do you want it to have been about?

If getting better ideas is about letting go, what would you do differently? How would you behave at work? How would you approach your current projects? Would you treat people differently? Would it make a difference at home? Do you think your partner or friends would notice?

We all have a 'mask' that we put on when we're at work. The clothes we wear, what we choose to reveal about ourselves, the stories we tell or don't tell – these all make up our public image. There's nothing wrong with this. If you're going to a meeting, wearing a suit can be a way of showing respect for the person you're meeting. It can help give you confidence and serve as a type of armour. This is OK. When you're running your own business and are really out there on a limb, it can be comforting to have these types of buffers around you.

When we're ourselves, however, we're more creative. We're free from the limits that we often put on ourselves. We're able to think openly and expansively. The sky's the limit.

Have you ever wondered why people are more creative outside their work environment? I recently worked with a team of bankers who agreed unanimously that they were about the most uncreative bunch you could hope to find. It sounded like a great challenge! When we started talking further, I asked how they spent their weekends. The responses ranged from sky diving, to gardening, to seriously good cooking. When I asked if they didn't think these were creative pursuits, they were sceptical and unconvinced. They were no Van Gogh or Harold Pinter, they said – both truly creative people. They were not going to be fobbed off with a soft soap. It's true that some people are more creative than others and the Van Goghs and Pinters of the world are pretty high on that scale. But that doesn't mean that if we aren't operating at that level, we're just a creativity-free zone.

Creativity is a skill and with a little practice anyone can learn to think creatively. What's not creative about nurturing a garden and watching it develop and grow? Making fantastic food – without the help of a recipe book – requires skill and a flair that many of us aspire to. Every one of the banking team spent their free time involved in genuinely creative pursuits. Yet when they walked through the front door of the office, they left all that behind. It was almost as if they took their creativity off with their coats on the way in, and picked it up again on the way home. The result of this was that instead of giving their all to their work, they were operating well below par.

In order to be creative, you have to let yourself go. In many ways, creative thinking is the opposite of logical thinking. It's a relaxed, spontaneous way of thinking. Don't take yourself too seriously. Be prepared to be silly, have a laugh at yourself. To get into your creative flow, your whole body and mind has to let go.

Exercise

- Remember a time when you have been creative either at home or at work.
- What did you do? This can be anything from cooking a meal without using a recipe to coming up with a solution to an issue at work.
- Where were you when you came up with the solution?
- What was it about this that made it easier?
- How do you feel you can be most creative? With others or on your own?

- What is it about this that allows you to come up with ideas?
- How can you use this knowledge to help you in future?
- Can you be your true self at work? If yes, why? If not, why not?

Look back at your journal and read what you've written. Research suggests that writing down your thoughts is a useful way of connecting with your subconscious self. When you understand more about your subconscious it tends to mean you're calmer and therefore have a greater chance of being more creative.

THE CREATIVE PROCESS

Challenge: Write down five things people don't know about you and ask for everyone in the team to add theirs. Then post them up around the office.

> There are dozens of creative approaches and techniques you could adopt, but for me the process is, and should be, simple. I have used this process many times and seen first hand the results it yields. The bottom line is, it works!
>
> Much research has been carried out into the way we use our brains by current thinkers like Tony Buzan and Robert Ornstein. They believe that true brain power is about engaging with all sides of life, not just facts and figures – using both the right and left side of your brain.

Right and left brain

In 1981, the Nobel Prize for Medicine was awarded to the American neuropsychologist Roger Sperry. After a lifetime of research, he discovered that the two sides of the brain are distinctly different. They have different characteristics and therefore perform two very different jobs.

The left side of the brain deals with logic, words, numbers, analysis, lists and sequences. It uses logic and rationale to approach a problem and reach a decision. It is fast, efficient and great when there is just one answer. The right side, on the other hand, deals with colour, rhythm, imagination, music, dimension, intuition and spatial awareness. 'Right brain' thinking can feel inefficient or indulgent, but it's free flowing and great for generating ideas.

Sperry discovered that if one side of the brain is particularly well developed, it reduces your ability to use the other side. However, if the less-developed side is put to work along with the stronger side, the total performance is hugely enhanced.

It's no wonder we need a little help to fine-tune our creative side: our society and our education system value left-brain analytical, logical thinking much more than imaginative, intuitive right-brain thinking. At school, we are taught the importance of focusing on facts and being accurate. This black and white distinction clearly fits into the left side of the brain. In fact, after pre-school, there is little importance placed on any of the activities that occur on the right side.

When I was at school, there was no room for music lessons in the normal curriculum, so for those of us wanting to learn music and take music O-level, as it was then, pupils and teachers stayed late for classes. This seemed perfectly normal to me at the time, but in hindsight it's a clear demonstration of the kind of low priority schools generally give to creative studies. And I don't think my school was unusual. On the up-side, at least it offered pupils the opportunity to study music, but it certainly wasn't considered in the same league as mathematics, English or sciences.

Because most of us have been through this type of school system, most of us have a far more developed left brain than right brain. The good news, as Sperry and Ornstein discovered, is that by tapping into the less-used right side of the brain, our overall performance will improve. We don't have to use just one side or the other in isolation; we can use both.

Tony Buzan, who has written numerous books on brain activity and creativity, believes that humans use less than 1% of the one trillion (one million, million) cells in our brains. We are clearly an untapped resource, so there has to be room for improvement!

The creative process

The process is gloriously simple.

THOUGHT + RELAXATION + IDEAS = ACTION

Thought

Spend some time thinking about your challenge, whether it's coming up with a new product, thinking of a new marketing push, or attracting the right type of job candidates for a vacancy at your company.

To get the ball rolling, ask yourself as many questions as you need to be completely clear about what you want to achieve. There's nothing worse than discovering along the way that you're working on the wrong issue. Time spent thinking up-front will pay dividends all the way through. For example, if you're going to launch a new product, do you know exactly what you're going to produce and how, what the market is, what the demand is, what the production costs and lead times are?

- Do you know all the relevant facts?
- What information would help you get to a better solution?
- Who do you need to talk to?
- What do you need to research?

Remember the old adage 'if you always do what you have always done, you always get what you've always got'. If you want to get to a new solution you need to try different techniques.

Creative questions to ask yourself:

- Take a famous person or brand and ask how they would approach something. For example, how would the different Spice Girls manage their time? Posh would get someone in to do it for her, Sporty would go to the gym and figure it out; what would Ginger, Baby and Scary Spice do? What can you learn from this?

   Or what would Apple do in this situation? Perhaps they would strip the situation down to the absolute basics. Make it as simple as possible – no clutter, no unnecessary parts, just the essentials.

- How do I normally approach this issue? Write it down on the left-hand side as bullet points. On the right-hand side, write down the opposite of each bullet point.

   e.g. How do I attract the best candidates for a current vacancy?

   I would normally:
   - advertise in a relevant trade magazine
   - use recruitment companies
   - employ people on short-term contracts
      Opposite these, instead I could:
   - invest the money I would have spent on advertising on developing the people we have
   - ask for referrals from friends and former colleagues from within our own ranks

- employ non-contracted staff (such as temps or freelancers) to cut down on our outgoings
- If you had all the time and resources you could possibly want, how would you solve this problem? How can you apply this to your current situation?
- If you could wipe the slate clean, what would you do? What can you do to change this situation?
- What advice would you give to someone in the same situation as you?
- What ideas has this given you?

Relaxation

We receive more stimuli in a week than our ancestors did in a lifetime! We are surrounded by background sounds all day long: phones ringing in the office and on our commute to and from work, e-mails pinging on our PCs, adverts flicking on bill boards, you name it – and there's very little escape.

So if we know that the creative process happens in three stages, once you've done the initial thinking and considered all the aspects of your challenge, the next stage is time out to relax and distil the information.

The benefits of 'sleeping on it' have now been proved by scientists. Researchers from the University of Pennsylvania found that the best way to make sense of and remember new information is to get some quality sleeping time. If sleeping isn't an option – and it's not likely that you can wander off for nap in the middle of the day when you've got a business to run – give yourself some time out. When you're at work, a five-minute walk round the block will work wonders. If time constraints aren't too pressing and you have the luxury to think things through overnight, play around with the issue in your head while you're cooking dinner or in the gym and then put it out of your mind when you go to bed. This combination of what's called fast and slow creativity – wrestling mentally with the issue and then taking some completely switch-off relaxation time – is a mighty combination to help you get to great ideas.

Ideas

You are now in a strong place and ideas will start to flow. I'm not talking big, life-changing ideas that appear like magic out of the blue; I'm talking about making connections, putting thoughts together in such a way that they start to do something different. For example, Post-it™ Notes were born from glue that didn't work as well as expected. Someone realised that the adhesive could be used in a different way, as temporary glue. The pyramid tea bag is still a tea bag, but revolutionised the market. It was new and generated excitement, but all that had changed was the shape. Toilet Duck took an innovative packaging idea that got under the rim and turned the loo cleaner market on its head!

Your ideas could be about addressing your weaknesses head-on. Starbucks have been strongly criticised for their global dominance, the closure of many independent cafés and their policy towards farming communities in developing countries. Their response was to come up with their own strong community focus, selling fair trade coffee and hosting local community programmes for children.

Remember that, in fact, there are very few *completely original* ideas. But that doesn't matter: what creativity at work is about is mixing up the pot, putting existing ideas together and seeing what comes out. That's what creates the magic.

Action

I mentioned above that the process is simple . . . and it is! The challenging bit, however, is making it happen and translating good ideas into new products, services or processes. Having great ideas is pointless unless you do something with them. Creativity in business is only powerful if you act on it and few companies can afford to be creative for the sake of it. Think about focused creativity that leads to results.

Creativity is about breaking patterns and norms that we all have. If you are the creative powerhouse in your business, then you need to bring it to life and make sure that it does result in a real improvement or innovation. Think laterally about how you communicate it to others. Avoid e-mail. It's a creativity killer and has become so over-used in most businesses that staff either ignore messages or just scan-read them and often miss key information.

To avoid this, think of alternative ways of communicating what you want to say. If today marks a line in the sand and a new, more innovative way of working, tease people that a change is coming. For example, you could design a little desk sticker with a creative symbol like a light bulb and with your chosen date on display to let people know 'creativity starts here!'. Deliver them to everyone's desk before they arrive at work to arouse their curiosity and so that they'll know that something is about to change. Then gather everyone together and explain your plans and what you want to do. Ask the team for their suggestions and input and follow up on their ideas.

Use wall space – especially the loos – to inspire people with new emerging trends or interesting innovative ideas you've come across or read about. Encourage your people to add to these with their own thoughts. At Clear, the ideas company where I work, the loos are a constant source of new and changing information – anything from interesting articles to requests for help on a particular project. It makes them much more stimulating places to be! Everyone goes there and you have a captive audience . . .

10 tips to encourage right-brain thinking

1 Draw with your non-dominant hand

Try drawing with the hand you don't normally use to write with. If you are right-handed, pick up a pen with your left hand and see what happens (and vice versa). If you allow your instinct to control your hand, you're allowing the right side of your brain to take over. Small children are ambidextrous for some time and they alternate freely between one hand and the other. According to the children's health expert, Dr Carol Cooper, there often seems to be no real preference until they reach the age of four. Whether you are left or right handed (also called 'laterality') is related to which side of the brain is dominant, though it is not a simple right- or left-side link.

2 Visualisation

Close your eyes and imagine you are somewhere else. I often imagine that I am on a beach or on a country walk. Paint a picture in your mind of where you are, what you see, what you smell, the sounds that are around you. Who else is there? What are they doing? Are you part of this or simply observing? This is a great way to relieve tension, which is a barrier to creativity. If you're stressed and under pressure, you won't be able to think creatively or use the right side of your brain. Your imagination is part of your right brain, so allowing yourself to go somewhere else, even for a few seconds, can help get you back on track.

Jack Black, creator of a personal development programme called Mindstore, is dedicated to encouraging left-brain thinkers to use the right, more intuitive, side of the brain. He has created a visualisation exercise where you imagine a house on the right bank of a river and design it according to your own specifications – what he calls your 'house on the right bank'. Inside the house, there are rooms which are intended for specific purposes: one for managing stress and giving you energy, one in which you can learn to sleep better and improve your creativity and problem-solving abilities, and so on. The idea is that most of us need help accessing the more creative side of our brain. If you visualise this in a metaphorical way by picturing a house built on the right-hand side of a river bank, then it will help you tap into your right brain and encourage ideas and creative thought.

3 Write down your thoughts

Putting pen to paper every day and letting your thoughts flow uncensored is another way to exercise your right brain. Writers use this technique to get in the creative flow and free up their thinking. Buy yourself a notebook and spend five minutes a day writing whatever comes to mind. Or if it's easier, tap away on your computer and keep an electronic journal. Your ability to think creatively will greatly improve.

4 Talk about things

Often situations that feel complicated when you're at the centre of them can feel extraordinarily simple to someone a little distance away. If there's an issue you're struggling with, it's common not to be able to see the wood for the trees. Stepping away from the problem can be a useful way to explore new thinking. Discuss your challenge or problem with someone who has no links to it all — partners, children, colleagues who aren't involved. They're likely to give you a fresh perspective based on their experience and this may open up the possibility of a new avenue for you to explore.

5 Think of something invigorating

Think of invigorating experiences that refresh you and that have the power to recharge your batteries. Make a list of these, anything from a massage to having a welcome cup of tea.

Have a think about what it is about these experiences that has this effect and jot down your thoughts. Thinking how these characteristics could be used to give new impetus to your challenge is a great right-brain activity.

6 Listen to music

Listening to music is a great form of relaxation, so choose something that will enable you to 'escape'. Classical music or music without lyrics is especially good for this: it allows the brain to tune into a different wavelength and uses the right side of your brain.

7 Use colour

When making notes, writing or doodling in your notebook, use different colours to bring everything to life. It will also serve as a memory aid as the colours will help you retain what you've written.

8 Drink lots of water

Thinking is thirsty work. Whatever you're working on, make sure you drink plenty of water. It keeps your brain hydrated and functioning well. Also avoid drinking too much caffeine as it has the opposite effect: after a short burst, your energy levels dip and you'll be dehydrated.

9 Relax and meditate

Breathing techniques are a great way to help you relax and free up your thinking. Try to find five minutes a couple of times a day to do this. Whatever location you choose, close your eyes for a few minutes and focus on your breathing. Take deep breaths and feel yourself relax and drift away from what's going on around you. With a little practice you'll be able to do this in the middle of a busy office or on the train. This is an effective technique to restore some balance after a hard day in the office – it's often difficult to be the person you'd like to be when you walk through your front door. If you have children, it's especially important that you have some energy left for them after work has taken its toll. A short relaxation exercise on the way home can be intensely powerful. I recommend you try to do this every day in order to recharge your energy levels before arriving home.

Jack Black suggests you visualise a shower so that you will literally feel refreshed and revived as though you've just had a lovely long wash. Imagine a shower head with a warm flow of spring water. The water is gently running through your hair and over every inch of your body. Black suggests focusing on any negatives that have been building up throughout the day, like anger, pettiness or fear, and imagining them all being washed away and down the plughole.

I've used this exercise on the train or bus on my way home from work and the results have been amazing. If you drive to work, spend a couple of minutes in the car before you set off for home or when you pull up at your house and try this. It really is possible to feel as if you've just stepped out of the shower. At the end of the day, it will ensure you're in a much better place to enjoy the rest of your evening. In fact, you can use it at any time of day when you need a quick injection of energy before tackling your creative challenge afresh.

10 Write a poem

Did you ever write poetry when you were at school? Children from a very young age enjoy the sound and rhythm of nursery rhymes and at this age many of us are at our creative peak. Children's authors like Julia Donaldson write books that are rich with rhyme. For instance, in *The Gruffalo* (Macmillan, 1999), she begins:

'A mouse took a stroll through the deep dark wood. A fox saw the mouse and the mouse looked good.'

Put pen to paper and let your imagination run riot. Don't worry if it doesn't make it sense – invent new words and write whatever springs to mind. Here are a few lines from J A Lindon's poem 'Sink Song' which might encourage you!

Scouring out the porridge pot
Round and round and round!

Out with all the scraith and scoopery,
Lift the eely ooly droopery,
Chase the glubbery slubbery gloopery
Round and round and round!

Out with all the doleful dithery,
Ladle out the slimy slithery,
Hunt and catch the hithery thithery,
Round and round and round!

Out with all the obbly gubbly,
On the stove it burns so bubbly,
Use the spoon and use it doubly,
Round and round and round.

Keep your journal with you and try this exercise over breakfast or on your way to work – it will warm up your brain as well as hopefully make you smile in the process.

4 EXERCISING YOUR CREATIVE MUSCLE

'Too often people deem themselves non-creative because they fail to live up to the unrealistic myth that true innovators generate brilliant, radically different, fully formed ideas. Breaking free from this myth is the first step in realising one's creative potential.'

Anne Miller, director of The Creativity Partnership

Brainstorming and other creative exercises

Challenge: Pick up a newspaper or magazine and glance through the horoscopes. Circle anything that catches your eye that you find interesting. Have a go at using these words or phrases to help you with your problem.

Creativity is about coming up with new and exciting ideas to help you tackle challenges more effectively. In order to get there, you need to think expansively in as broad a context as possible, often way beyond the immediate problem you're facing. If an idea sounds as if it's come from outer space, don't dismiss it immediately; instead, ask yourself if there's a germ of something that you could build on.

Often, great ideas start off sounding pretty outlandish and don't make sense on paper. For example Persil's advertising campaign 'Dirt is good' turned the usual view that dirt is a problem for parents on its head. The idea was based on the insight that children learn about life through making mistakes, falling off, getting dirty and parents want to encourage children to experience life full on. The campaign led to an increase in sales for Persil's manufacturer Unilever.

What starts out as a humble little seed of an idea can have the power really to make a difference when it takes hold. These early foundations of creativity are part of the process for you to be able to 'sell' your ideas to other people later. Telling others the story of how the idea started, came together and created a great result can be a powerful argument when you're looking for support down the line. Remember the journey you went on with your idea and share it with others at a relevant moment.

In the meantime, here are some techniques to exercise your creative muscle!

Many of these are group exercises. However, they can work even if your group is smaller than the suggested optimum number. If you work in a very small team, you might want to consider inviting some 'guests' to contribute to your session – members of another small business perhaps; you could always return the favour on another occasion.

1 Brainstorming (suitable for small groups of four to eight people)

Be clear about what you want to achieve

Even though the joy of brainstorming is that it allows people to 'freewheel' and be creative in the way they think about things, it will only be an effective means of tackling a problem if you're very specific about what you want to achieve. This doesn't mean you should suggest a potential outcome (see the box below) as this would set limits on the participants' ideas

Brainstorming or analysis?

Before you go too far down the brainstorming route, make sure that this is the right way to tackle your problem. Brainstorming is best done when you need to innovate and create a range of ideas. If you already have some possible solutions to a problem but just don't know which one to pick, it's probably best to hold an analysing session, in which you work out the pros and cons of each one separately. Brainstorming may simply confuse the issue by producing even more potential solutions, none of which are more compelling than those you have already.

even before you start, but do be sure of what your overall goal is and roughly how you want to get there.

Find the right mix of people

First of all, be sure that you're the best person (or 'facilitator') to be leading the meeting. Good facilitators have the right mix of enthusiasm, knowledge, tact and team-leading skills so they'll be able to make sure that the brainstorming group is pulling together during the session. When you run your own business, it can be incredibly tempting to want to step in and take control of all aspects of it, but you need to be realistic about your own skills. Don't be afraid to ask a colleague to run the session and facilitate if you think you might not be the right person for this job. In fact, sometimes you might find it helpful to have someone with some distance from the issue under discussion, as they'll be able to be more objective.

You might also find it useful to ask a wider variety of people to attend than you would for a standard in-house meeting. Obviously you'll need people there who know your business well, but think carefully about other colleagues or contacts who – even though they might not work with you every day – can bring their talents or experience to bear on the issue being discussed.

Pick the right place

Good venues for brainstorming have lots of natural light and are spacious enough to allow the participants to move round comfortably. Here are some other aspects worth considering:

- ■ Try to find a room that is quiet and that you can close the door to so other colleagues aren't disturbed. If your budget stretches to hiring a room outside your normal office building, so much the better – it will help foster the idea that you're trying to get away from established thinking and procedures.
- ■ Make sure you have a whiteboard and plenty of paper and pens so that ideas can be noted.
- ■ Keep the atmosphere as informal as you can by avoiding rigid seating plans; if you need a table in the room, try to get a round one so that no one's seated at the head of it.
- ■ Ask everyone to turn off their mobile phones so that they won't interrupt the meeting.

Stay flexible

At the beginning of the meeting, clarify again just what it is that you're brainstorming so that everyone's clear about it. This first part of the session is the one when you are throwing the issue open to everyone's differing creative approaches, so stay flexible and don't dismiss any idea out of hand.

If you're the facilitator:

- Make sure everyone joins in.
- Don't criticise suggestions that you think are outlandish: not only will you dampen the mood of the meeting, but you'll risk dismissing what could be (after some development) the very idea that gets you the ideal solution.
- Make a note of all suggestions on the whiteboard, flip chart, or large pieces of paper you're using to record potential solutions; having these clearly visible around the room will help spark off other ideas.
- More is definitely more at this stage: encourage everyone to come up with as many ideas as they possibly can.

Try to keep the momentum up during this phase of the brainstorming by being actively enthusiastic and positive. If you sense that energy is flagging, give people a measurable but eminently achievable goal: 'Let's think of five more ideas before we break for lunch', for example.

As the session draws to a close, thank everyone for his or her time and collaboration and let them know what will happen next. If you'd like them to read over the minutes so you can start isolating the best ideas, announce when you expect them to be ready and stick to that date.

Whittle down the ideas into a practical solution

Once you have your list of ideas, rank them in order of practicality. Will any of them really work in the cold light of day? If you are asking the brainstorming team from the meeting to help you evaluate the ideas, ask them to plump for their top five (maximum) ideas, rejecting those that are just too off the wall.

Once you have compiled a 'master' top five list, look at each option carefully, working out:

- costs
- time scales
- competition
- legal issues
- negative factors

2 Mind Mapping (this exercise can be carried out on your own or in small groups of up to four people)

Mind Maps™ are good when you have too many thoughts whirling around in your head and need to get them down on paper. They're also useful if there are lots of different angles to your challenge and you need to have an overview of them. Use Mind Maps with your own staff and external clients or customers so that you're clear about what their issues are. For example, there may be issues going on behind the scenes that you're not aware of up front. Using this technique can help you uncover some of these issues which will, in turn, help you tackle the challenge from a more realistic perspective.

Make sure you have plenty of A3 paper to hand, and then write your challenge in the middle of a sheet. Note down all the thoughts that spring from your central challenge, as well as any further connections or ideas you spot or see as you're going along.

Eventually you'll end up with a big spider-like diagram. When you're ready, sit back, read through it and make a note of any emerging themes. Do any of the ideas fit together? Organise your thoughts into the topics that have emerged during the exercise.

3 Story boarding (suitable for groups of around six people, but it can work for larger teams if they're divided into smaller groups)

Storyboarding is a good technique when you have a complicated problem with no clear idea of what the optimum outcome is. For example, if you want to extend your range of products but are unsure of the direction to go in, this way forward is great.

Dove have certainly benefited from story boarding. Part of Lever Fabergé, the company started out manufacturing a soap bar, the key benefit of which was that it was one-quarter moisturiser. They wanted to extend their range, but were unclear about how to take the brand forward. Eventually they discovered that a significant percentage of women were frustrated and alienated by the image of beauty represented in glossy magazines. This insight led to a dramatic rise in new product ideas and profit when they began a campaign for 'real beauty'. They used real women in their advertising rather than models and suddenly opened up a wealth of new opportunities to enter the market in most female personal care products – all of which were advertised using 'airbrushed', 'perfect' images of women.

Give everyone in the group a pack of Post-it™ notes. Ask them to write their ideas about your challenge on the Post-its™ with one idea per note. After 2–3 minutes, stop the exercise and look for themes among the ideas. Group the ideas into different categories and clearly label them. Then divide everyone into smaller groups and ask each couple or trio to work on a different category. This is about refining the ideas and looking at what actions you need to take to move forward. Who do you need to talk to? Who is likely to sponsor the idea within your organisation? What do you need to do next to make it happen?

> Make sure you end up with no more than eight themes. You're looking for quality here, not quantity. If you have more than this, ask the group to vote for their favourite in order to eliminate the others.

4 Storytelling (suitable for groups of three to four people)

Storytelling is a powerful tool to harness creative thought and encourage people to get behind your idea. It's also fun – people like stories and with practice you can become a great storyteller. It works as an exercise because it lifts you beyond the small details that often get in the way of new ideas.

Think about what you want to achieve with your challenge. For example, let's say you want to attract fantastic talent to work in your small business. Divide everyone into groups of three to four people. Then ask them what the future might look like once you've solved your challenge and have the most talented team of individuals working for you. What will you and your business be famous for? What will the newspapers say about your organisation? Design the front page of *The Times* or the *Daily Mail* with a suitable headline about the kind of business you are.

Use simple, clear, provocative language to make sure you really get your message across. Spend some time thinking about the message you want people to take away with them – and especially your top line.

Journalists are taught to start their stories with the crux of the issue. If you're writing a story for the 6 o'clock news, there's no point in burying the best bit half-way through: your audience will have switched off in every sense. The 'top line' is incredibly important for journalists: it can make or break their story and most agonise for a long time to make sure they get it right. It's the hook that draws people in and makes them want to listen – it conveys the relevant information and leaves the audience wanting to know more.

Bring your story to life by encouraging the group really to think about what life will be like when you've solved your challenge and you have the best talent in the market on your pay roll – when recruiters say you're the number one choice for candidates in your field.

5 Show starter (suitable for groups of four to five people)

When you need fresh stimulation, introducing a bit of theatre will always generate some new perspectives. Divide the group into small teams of no more than four to five people. Give them 10 minutes to put together a sketch acting out the challenge they're facing. For example, if you want to drive up demand for your product, one person takes the role as the research and development engineer, another as head of sales, someone will play your customer, another your main competitor etc. Ask each team to act out their sketch before the whole group, improvising the conversations that would take place as they go along.

> At the end of the exercise ask each team to give feedback on what they learnt during the exercise. Keep a record of all the lessons and discuss with the wider group what practical steps you can take to action them.

6 Your inner artist (suitable for groups of 10–12 people divided into pairs)

Give each member of the team a selection of pens, pencils and any other artistic materials you like and then ask them to draw a picture of the problem they're facing.

Next, ask each person to talk through their picture to the wider group and explain the significance of what's been drawn on the page. This can be an enlightening process for the artist as well as for the group.

Drawing is a right-brain activity and stimulates the creative side of the brain.

> This exercise works well carried out in pairs. You can discuss the issues you're facing with your partner and then illustrate them on a page. People often feel more comfortable doing this exercise if they can talk about their anxieties first to get them out of their system! It often helps then get over the barrier of putting pen to paper.

7 Other worlds (suitable for groups of four to eight people)

Fresh thinking is fundamental to creativity and the best way to achieve it is to have fresh experiences. Bring in a selection of books, newspapers and magazines on a wide variety of subjects. You can even add to your list different music, fabric samples, different teas or spices – anything that stimulates the senses and gets you thinking. Then ask the group to spend some time looking through the stimuli to find solutions to the problem they face. If you have time, send them out to make connections between what they see in the outside world and their challenge. The aim of the exercise should be for everyone to come up with at least two new ideas that have been generated from what they've seen or read.

Make sure you're very specific about your goal at the outset, or you won't get any practical results at the end.

8 'Fake rules' (suitable for groups of 10–12 people divided into smaller teams)

In advance of the session, draw up a list of 'fake rules' that could apply to your business. For example, if you're a small specialist crisp manufacturer, your rules could be that the government has decided to ban all confectionery and snack foods in a bid to reduce childhood obesity; that you must be over 18 years of age to use this product; that this must be kept refrigerated after opening; that you must avoid contact with the skin etc.

Each team pulls out an envelope with a 'fake rule' in it and has five minutes to apply it to their challenge. Allow each team to have six rounds of fake rules to brainstorm ideas.

Then allow the teams 10 minutes to sum up their ideas before presenting them back to the rest of the group.

Make sure the rules are fairly general and that they can be applied to your industry. They don't have to be realistic – in fact, the odder the better to stretch thinking and really give everyone's creative muscles a good work-out!

5 UNDERSTANDING HOW CREATIVE PEOPLE TICK

> Challenge: Try moving your work space – even for a few hours. If you have a laptop, move it to another part of the office. A change of scene will shift your thinking and give you a different perspective on the issues of the day. It's also useful for building your relationships with a different group of people.

'Insanity is trying the same thing again and again and expecting a different result.' Albert Einstein

> When I started thinking about this book, I asked myself who really stood out in my mind because of the creative way they work and conduct their lives. You'll have your own list of people you know, have worked with or read about who'll have influenced you and your work. I've picked a few of the people who've

inspired me and who I believe have experiences that have a real impact on small businesses, because that's the arena in which most of these people started off their business life.

The people featured in this book now run (or have run) very different kinds of companies, but there's one thing on which they're all agreed: their success hinges on a vision. A vision provides a greater purpose and requires people to think beyond the financial value of the company. If it's inspirational, a vision can create an opportunity for people to develop as they move towards it. It keeps morale high.

This often involves letting go of the reins and allowing others to have their say. By asking people for their input, you're allowing them to be part of the decision process and part of the vision for the future. According to Graham Lindsay, head of retail at LloydsTSB, 'Vision is the most valuable asset you have. Unless you have clearly articulated your vision to your people, they will feel like they're going nowhere. People alone without vision won't work.'

Vision

The world of banking has been widely regarded as traditional and inflexible – not the place you'd automatically go looking for creativity. Yet that's exactly what First Direct were demonstrating when they came up with their 24-hour banking service with no branches: it was the first in the UK.

When First Direct entered the market in 1989, very few people had access to the Internet (these days we spend more time online than we do watching television), so initially all dealings were handled on the phone. The company realised immediately that communication was going to be key. What they wanted to create was a simple, friendly and flexible service that could compete with face-to-face contact on the high street. They recruited from people-focused occupations like teaching and nursing rather than the conventional choice of banking. And they invested heavily in training to ensure that everyone was able to live and breathe their brand. They used direct mail with a warm, easy, conversational style to build strong one-to-one relationships with their customers.

Their success speaks for itself: they took on 500,000 customers in the first 15 months and have achieved 90% customer satisfaction and 97% customer retention since. And they appear in lists of the best companies to work for.

Here are eight people who had a vision and then acted on it. All of them come from very different backgrounds and some had virtually no experience of business when they set up their companies. What they have in common, though, is an idea that they believed in.

Greg Dyke

When Greg Dyke took over as Director-General of the BBC, his vision was to turn the BBC into 'the most creative organisation in the world'. But the way it had been run previously was anything but creative: there was widespread dislike and distrust of management and an overwhelming feeling that the BBC's accomplishments were reached in spite of, rather than thanks to, the management.

On the day he left the BBC in 2004, staff waved placards saying 'Bring back Greg' outside Television Centre and across the country. Many were in tears. I was one of thousands of staff who signed their name on a full-page petition in the *Daily Telegraph*, paid for by staff themselves. The advert supported Greg Dyke and confronted the BBC governor's decision to fire him in the wake of the Hutton Report.

Rewind four years to when he took on the job. Dyke made a point of talking to every member of staff. He asked each person the same two questions. 'What do we need to change in order to improve our service?' and 'What can I do to make your life better?'

For the most part, what people made were pretty straightforward, sensible requests that could easily be put into practice at little cost.

Greg Dyke tells a story he read at his father's funeral about the kind of man his father was. He said he always stopped to talk to the road sweeper. His father had no time for self-important people who thought they were better than everyone else. His view was that everyone deserved respect. Dyke believes that when you have this simple certainty as your guide, everything else will fall into place.

In his autobiography, *Inside Story* (HarperCollins, 2004), he sets out what he sees are the necessary criteria for running a successful creative organisation. The key points are paraphrased below.

Be yourself

The most inspiring, motivated, successful individuals all have one thing in common, in Dyke's view. They don't pretend to be anyone else – they aren't afraid to be themselves. When you are given the responsibility of leadership, it's because of who you are. It's madness then to start adopting the behaviours of someone you think you should be – your idea of what a leader should be. People will see it for what it is straight away, and anyway, it's much too stressful to spend your time worrying about your 'act' rather than the job in hand. Confidence and self-belief are key to this, and Dyke believes that by having faith in yourself, you will reap the rewards.

The importance of communication

It's impossible to emphasise this enough. Walk into any organisation and the vast majority of them will tell you that good, effective communication is what they aspire to.

According to Dyke, it doesn't have to be complicated. 'People working in the organisation are more likely to support you and what you are trying to achieve if they feel they are involved in a two-way conversation with you.' In an organisation like the BBC with 30,000 members of staff, this is no mean feat – for many organisations, it's hard enough to achieve even when all your people work under the same roof and in the same building.

The way Greg Dyke achieved it was through a few simple techniques that made a big impact. For example, he sent regular e-mails, always signed 'Greg'. He made internal broadcasts and question and answer sessions that were transmitted live in BBC buildings around the country and could be watched on internal monitors. He wrote frequently in the in-house magazine. His tone was upfront, direct and conversational and without any management jargon.

Honesty is the only policy

Don't be afraid to hold up your hands and say 'I made a mistake': your staff will like and respect you more for it. When the BBC tried to change the expenses payments, there was a backlash from staff and the decision was reviewed. The conclusion was that the reforms were too much and the plan was changed. As leader, Dyke took responsibility for the decision and admitted the mistake on the front page of the in-house magazine, a gesture which he credits with making him new friends.

Lead by example

Dyke is a firm believer in practising what you preach: the old 'do as I say not as I do' mantra won't work. If there are behaviours you want your team to adopt at work, lead the way and adopt them yourself first. For example, if you want to encourage your staff to share ideas and mix more with each other, then you have to do the same. There's no point in sitting in your ivory tower and waiting for it to happen. Dyke's policy was always to collect his own lunch from the staff canteen. He could have sent someone else to fetch it, but his presence, queuing up with other members of staff sent an important message that he was one of the team and on the same side.

Persuade those around you that their talents know no bounds

This boils down to motivation and is one of the most important creative tools of all, as Dyke sees it. He feels that if you can convince an individual that they can achieve results way beyond their wildest expectations, you'll have created a little piece of magic.

For Dyke, the reality is that we're all capable of great things. The author Marianne Williamson's words, used by Nelson Mandela for his inauguration speech, hit the nail on the head. 'Our deepest fear is not that we are inadequate. Our deepest fear is that we are powerful beyond measure. It is our light, not our darkness, that most frightens us.'

We all respond better when we know others believe in us. Let your people shine and enjoy the results.

Show your people you care

In the profit and results driven world of business, genuinely caring for your people may seem a bit of an impossibility, but Dyke feels that adopting a genuine attitude of caring will allow you to stand head and shoulders above your competitors. For example, an engineering company I know shows its people it cares in a couple of simple ways. No one is allowed to work on their birthday and overtime is against the rules. Since these policies were introduced, profits have soared – people want to give their all.

Breakthrough moment: Susie Willis

In 2005, Susie Willis saw a gap in the market for healthy, organic baby food. She set up Plum Baby, making purées of super foods like blueberries and spinach that appealed to babies and parents alike. It's been a big success: at the end of 2007, her company had a turnover of £3.5 million. One of the biggest hurdles she faces is fighting off the competition from big name brands. 'You have to be absolutely positive that your idea has as many identifiable ownership elements as possible,' she says. 'I know the competition have tried to copy us, but they've done it half-heartedly, and they can keep on trying. We keep on innovating, and that's what enables us to punch above our weight.'

James Dyson

Dyson inherits his vision from that great Briton, Isambard Kingdom Brunel. Brunel's confidence in his own abilities was so strong that the possibility of failure didn't ever seem to occur to him. James Dyson lived near one of Brunel's many achievements, the railway tunnel at Box on the outskirts of Bath. Set deep into the rolling hillside, the tunnel is an enormous feat of engineering and was designed so expertly that when the two sides met in the middle, they were mere millimetres apart.

Dyson says of his hero that when his own prospects looked bleak, he tried to hold on to something of Brunel's self-belief to see him through his darker days. So what does James Dyson put his success down to? Well apart from vision and a dogged determination, here are a few characteristics of the Dyson road to success.

Working for Dyson means making a vacuum cleaner on day one

From the most senior to the most junior member of the team, working for Dyson means being hands-on. So much so, each new recruit has to put together a Dyson cleaner from scratch. The thinking is that everyone will then understand the whole product even if they're only working on one particular section. They then get to take the machine home and test it out to see how they've fared!

Design pervades every part of the business

When the Dyson team moved into their new factory in Malmesbury, Wiltshire, the building was adapted dramatically. James's wife Deirdre designed the new interior colour scheme and they splashed out on expensive chairs for every employee. The offices were open-plan to encourage people to talk to each other. The idea was to make everyone aware of design and their part of the design process that was taking place right there.

It's everyone's responsibility to come up with ideas

The demarcation lines that organisations use for different departments are deliberately blurred at Dyson. Engineers and designers are not viewed there, as they are in some larger organisations, as being polar opposites. Staff are encouraged to come up with ideas not just in the area where they have direct involvement, but across other departments too. For example, it was a member of the service team's idea to put the helpline number on machine handles.

The importance of conversation

Memos are banned in Dyson's world and he doesn't have a good word to say about e-mails either. 'Dialogue is the founding principle for progress,' writes Dyson in his autobiography, *Against the Odds*. He believes that if you've got something to say, then say it: have a conversation.

You are what you wear

Dyson has an aversion to being taken for a businessman. As a designer, it's not surprising that he is particular about the image his company conveys, but this goes beyond style. He doesn't want his employees thinking like businessmen. 'I have no time for businessmen; they are suited pen pushers who have always endeavoured to stifle creativity.'

His aim is to encourage his employees to think their own thoughts rather than conform to any given pattern – to be free to challenge and think radical thoughts.

Unconventional is good

As well as not conforming to any dress code, Dyson's aim is to encourage his people to be deliberately different, even difficult. He believes that this will help individuals to think illogically rather than logically. Doing this yourself could help solve your own business challenges and those of your clients.

Breakthrough moment: Errol Damelin and Jonty Hurwitz

Currently listed as one of the top 20 start-ups in the UK, Wonga was set up by Errol Damelin and Jonty Hurwitz to change the way we think about banking and loans. Wonga uses technology like the Internet and mobile phones to offer customers immediate quick-fix loans that they then pay back over a month. It's an alternative to a credit card loan: up to £200 will immediately appear in your bank account once you have confirmed a date to repay the loan and agreed an interest rate. The pair say their biggest challenge has been dealing with a 'decrepit and outdated' banking system that has struggled with the concept of 'instant loans'.

Sahar Hashemi

In 1996, Sahar Hashemi and her brother Bobby opened an espresso bar called Coffee Republic. At the time, it was the first

American-style coffee bar in the UK. They had a vision to bring great tasting coffee to the British high street with the kinds of choices never before dreamt of this side of the Atlantic. In the mid-1990s, skinny, decaf, half caf with caramel and cream weren't options available in your average British café.

At the time, Sahar had spent a while in America and had seen at first hand the coffee craze that was sweeping the States. Bobby was working there as a financier and was also aware of the new breed of cafés. They were entrepreneurs with a vision which was to lead to a hugely successful business idea and the introduction of a new 'coffee culture' in Britain.

Twelve years on, it's hard to imagine life before the rise of coffee bars. Now they are on every street corner in every town and city, but when the first Coffee Republic opened its doors on a prime site in London, people didn't come. The idea was slow to take off. People walked past on their way to the office without calling in for their double espresso and skinny muffin.

Believe in your idea

Sahar puts their success down to determination and a solid belief that they had a great idea and were doing the right thing. There were many obstacles along the way and at one stage, her brother Bobby was set to give up. He still had the option of a good well-paid job to return to and when the prospects for Coffee Republic didn't look good, he almost abandoned the idea. He turned for advice to a good friend who he trusted and whose opinion he valued and was persuaded to stick it out. The company eventually grew to a chain with around 100 shops.

Persistence

You only ever hear of the success stories. For every successful entrepreneur there will be many who failed – those who gave up along the way.

I've been told that American banks are much more likely to lend money to people who have a few business failures behind them because it shows their persistence and determination to keep going and succeed. In his book *Think and Grow Rich* (Vermilion, revised edition, 2004), Napoleon Hill writes, 'There is a hidden guide whose duty is to test people through all sorts of discouraging experiences. Those who pick themselves up after defeat and keep on trying, arrive and then the world cries "Bravo! I knew you could do it!" The hidden guide lets no one enjoy great achievement without passing the persistence test.'

Take care of yourself

Being a successful entrepreneur is a long and often difficult road. It's important to pace yourself and look after yourself along the way. Sahar Hashemi recommends keeping fit, ensuring you keep going to the gym or doing whatever is your thing, along with the odd pampering session and treat to sustain you.

As the owner of a business, you're the public face of your company so it's important to present the right image. If you're not taking care of yourself this will send out the wrong signals, that perhaps your business is not quite under control.

Build a strong team around you

No matter how great your product is, if you don't have good people working with you then the customer experience will be in severe jeopardy. It's a well-known theory that people are a company's greatest asset, but they need to be the right people for the job – individuals who will sell your company for you when you're not there. In the case of Coffee Republic, it wasn't going to be possible for the owners to be in the coffee shop every day. And yet for every customer who walks through the door, the quality of their experience is determined by the exchange between them and the person serving them.

Finding the right people is imperative. In the early days of Coffee Republic, they weren't big enough to be able to train their own staff so the Hashemis decided to 'bootstrap'. The one company that they felt was delivering good customer service was the sandwich shop Pret a Manger. They were established and trained their staff well. Sahar blatantly decided to poach a few Pret staff by offering them a better salary to come and work for her. She felt that they could then train other members of staff and Coffee Republic would have the benefits of well-trained people without the expense of training them themselves. The idea initially backfired. When she and Bobby finally managed to summon up the courage to push a note with their phone number into the hands of a couple of unsuspecting Pret staff, they later discovered that they hardly spoke any English and so some serious language lessons were required!

Breakthrough moment: Richard Reed

The drinks company Innocent is an example of how a strong vision can be brought to life in every aspect of what a company does. Innocent was set up by three friends, Richard Reed, Adam Balon and Jon Wright, who left their well-paid office jobs to make fruit smoothies. Making fruit drinks wasn't their first business idea but they acted upon a gut feeling that if an easy way to keep healthy appealed to them, then it would appeal to others too. They all had busy jobs where they worked too late to do any physical exercise and where kebab shops were the only options for late-night food. Innocent's ethos is all about offering simple, fresh products that use natural ingredients. The company's HQ is called 'Fruit Towers', its vans are shaped like cows and it sponsors a free music festival called Fruitstock for 'nice people'. The people who work there identify with the brand and feel connected to it personally.

Richard Branson

Richard Branson is arguably the world's greatest entrepreneur. Yet when it comes to analysing the creative techniques that have led to his huge success, it's hard to get away from what boils down to the personality of the man himself. Branson has flair, colour and a shrewd business brain that has won him popularity in the media and with the public.

He has made a fortune by going against the grain and against the advice of the experts. Most of his decisions are based on instinct and he says all his acquisitions are in areas where he has a genuine interest. He has a love of fun and adventure which translates into all parts of his life, and this is coupled with an ability to motivate and inspire those around him.

Branson appears not to be intimidated by anyone or anything – however big. As he says, the dinosaurs didn't last forever either. Here are some of the factors that have enabled Branson to realise his vision of Virgin as one of the leading brand names of the 21st century.

Bravery

Saying Branson loves a challenge seems rather inadequate. Think of his many trips around the globe in flying machines of variable reliability. Think of his confrontation with British Airways. Taking on 'the world's favourite airline' that enjoyed government backing was never going to be an easy ride. Where Freddie Laker, Dan Air and others had failed, Branson succeeded.

When he left school, his headmaster's parting words were: 'Congratulations, Branson. I predict that you will either go to prison or become a millionaire.' Branson has an in-built confidence that he shares with many entrepreneurs, but perhaps with an appetite for risk that many don't. His self-confessed philosophy of 'Screw it, let's do it!' (the title of his book on lessons drawn from his experiences, in fact) isn't a business strategy you find frequently in the indexes of business tomes.

Do the unexpected

Branson's secret weapon is a pocket-sized notebook that he carries with him all the time. In it he writes down ideas – comments made by customers, passengers and staff. Details of every phone call he makes are also noted. In the evening, he goes through the comments and if there's a good idea, he puts it into practice. For example, a man he met on an airport bus suggested Virgin offer massages on their planes: it was done.

On his vision for Virgin, Branson says it changes all the time. A traditional approach might be to understand what you do well and stick to it. In Branson's view, that's a dangerous game. If you only run record shops and don't embrace change, when something like the Internet comes along, your business is in serious danger unless you're prepared to change.

Trust your instincts

In the early days of the computer games business, Virgin acquired the rights to distribute Sega games in Europe. In the late 1980s it would have been hard to predict the potential of that particular market, but Branson had noticed that much of his son's and daughter's time was spent in front of the television playing computer games. It was a good enough sign that it was worth getting involved. Three years later, the sales of Sega in Europe had soared from £2 million in 1988 to £150 million. But Branson became concerned that the bottom might fall out of the market. He noticed his son and daughter were spending much less time playing their computer games. This was the first warning sign and he decided to sell. Where marketing departments might well spend thousands of pounds tracking the market, Branson trusts his instincts when it comes to making his major business decisions.

PR

Richard Branson is a master of publicity. He regularly dresses up for the cameras – famously parading down the aisles of a Virgin Atlantic flight wearing a short air hostess skirt or sporting a wedding dress to promote Virgin Brides.

When launching Virgin Cola in America, he rigged up Coca Cola signs in Times Square with fireworks and launched an 'attack' from the Virgin Megastore across the square.

The impression Branson leaves you with is that he's game for pretty much any publicity stunt – giving the press something more interesting to print will not only give extra column inches to Virgin, but it's another opportunity for fun – something Branson values highly.

Fun at work

Time magazine writes 'Branson seems hell-bent on making sure that everybody, but everybody, is having as much fun as he is'.

On Virgin Atlantic's first flight, the plane was filled with conjurors and entertainers. Dozens of cases of champagne were loaded onto the flight. People danced in the aisles to hits of the time. The film *Airplane* was shown and the cabin crew started what became a tradition of handing out choc ices during the film.

I was once on board a Virgin flight and overheard the cabin crew discuss the opening of a new route to Dubai. They had, perhaps not surprisingly, all put their names down to work on that flight. It was clear it's not just the passengers who enjoy these events – it was obviously a big motivator for the staff too. Branson writes in his autobiography *Losing My Virginity* (Virgin Books, rev ed, 2007), 'Fun is at the core of how I like to do business . . . more than any other element, fun is the secret of Virgin's success'.

6
STRANGE IDEAS
THAT GET RESULTS

'Problems cannot be solved by thinking within the framework in which they were created.' Albert Einstein

Many of the most creative ways to work fly in the face of what we imagine is right. Some of them may seem obvious and good common sense. Others, quite the opposite.

Challenge: Grab the people who are standing next to you – half a dozen people if you are at work, your partner or children if you are at home and do the hokey cokey! How do you feel? Okay, you might feel a bit of an idiot, but I guarantee you won't be able to do it without smiling and happy people are more creative!

When you want a creative result, a good rule of thumb is to turn what is common practice on its head: do the opposite. Ask yourself: 'Why do we do it like this? What would happen if we did it differently?' Every organisation, big and small, can fall victim to entrenched routines and patterns of behaviour. Some of these are necessary to ensure the smooth daily running of the company – you need to do your invoices every week, naturally, order in the right parts or supplies regularly and so on – but most will benefit from a mighty good shake-up. Businesses that encourage new and fresh ideas will beat their rivals hands-down because of their ability to stay ahead of the game. Doing the same old thing every year isn't an option.

For the highly educated, highly skilled scribes who worked diligently transcribing bibles in the Middle Ages, the creation of the printing press marked the end of their livelihoods. When it arrived on the scene, they knew their days were numbered. It wasn't a case of being able to copy out more bibles faster: it didn't matter how many they did or how fast they worked, the scribes couldn't do it as efficiently as the machine.

I'm not saying it's easy. We are all guilty of falling into a safe, predictable rut. We set our alarm clock for the same time each morning. We get up and eat the same thing for breakfast. We go to work and go through more or less the same routine every day.

In order to think differently, you have to start acting differently. So the next time you're in a book shop, head for a section you've never ventured into before: pick a book on a subject you think you have no interest in and read it. Watch a television programme you'd never dream of bothering with normally. Take up singing lessons or learn a new language. Buy your weekly shopping at a market rather than your usual supermarket. Take a colleague you think you have nothing in common with out for lunch. Order something you've never heard of from the menu. Go on, you know you want to!

The great John Peel used to say on his Radio 4 programme, 'Home Truths', that he couldn't talk about his experiences if he wasn't having any. And the same is true here. To get somewhere new, you have to try something new. I'm not saying you have to do everything on the list, but start by doing something that takes you out of your normal routine and allows you to follow a different path.

In this chapter I describe some creative methods that I've experienced in action and that I've seen work well for those who used them. I'm sure some of these will trigger your own ideas and thoughts that you can add to the list. My creative methods are as follows:

1 Talk to people you don't like
2 Find random links
3 Identify your creative space
4 Break the rules
5 Go speed dating
6 Use job interviews to inspire you with new ideas
7 Learn from parallel industries
8 Create a senses box
9 Phone a friend
10 Imagine a corporate take-over

1 Talk to people you don't like

If you only associate with people who you feel comfortable around, you'll hear the same ideas that you've come up with already and just another person talking the same language as you. You won't be learning or experiencing anything new.

One of the difficulties with breaking this cycle is that it's human nature to want to associate with people who have the same views on life as we do. It helps cement our values and our view of the world. It is worth persevering with a shake-up, though. One of the fundamental principles at Clear, the ideas consultancy where I work, is 'better together', and it really works: when it comes to looking at a situation creatively, two brains are always better than one. Take a look at the situation around you. A five-minute conversation with the person sitting next to you, or better still someone at the opposite end of the office, can open up a whole new perspective and help you towards new ways of looking at a problem and new ways of solving it.

- Accept that sameness isn't a good thing.
- Talk to people of different ages – remember children are very creative. Be inspired by them and

consciously think what you could learn from their games and conversation.

■ The same is true of older people. Their views may well be different from yours – be open and willing to learn from their experience and different ideas.

■ If you feel uncomfortable in someone's company, ask yourself why this is. Is it just because they are different? Listen to what they have to say. What can you learn from them?

■ Encourage others to see the value in difference. You can't afford to keep doing everything in the same way and by the same token neither can they.

2 Find random links

It's hard to magic ideas out of nowhere. It's a bit like someone shouting, 'Be spontaneous! Now!'. We're more likely to panic and don a rabbit-in-the-headlights expression than actually to respond usefully. That's where stimulus comes in. Look around you. What can you see? Any stimulus can give you inspiration and take you to new and exciting places. Go into the garden, go for a walk, go upstairs. Find some random things and start to use them to help you with your issue. I've seen people get to amazing new ideas simply by taking random objects and starting to make connections.

The secret here is to have some fun with it. Ideas will flow more easily if you are in a relaxed state and aren't trying too hard. Explore your chosen stimulus and ask yourself what it makes you think about.

- Relax and don't take things too seriously.
- Not all stimuli work. Don't be put off if you pick something and you draw a blank. Move on. Find something else and try again.

3 Identify your creative space

Where are you most creative? Most of us have a place where we can work better, concentrate more and where we are best able to find solutions to our challenges. It doesn't matter if it's the shed, the garden, the kitchen or even in the bath – wherever you feel able to relax and think is the right place for you.

Walt Disney is known to have had a room in his house dedicated to thinking and ideas, a place where he was at his most creative. In fact, one of the famous stories told about Disney is what happened in the aftermath of a meeting that had gone badly – he'd been forced to give up control of Oswald the Rabbit, his most successful cartoon character at that time. On the train ride home, he began thinking about the mice that used to inhabit his old office and this triggered a new character in his imagination. Disney wanted to call this new creature 'Mortimer', but his wife persuaded him to call his new creation 'Mickey Mouse'. And so began the biggest success of his career.

Make it easy for yourself to tap into your creative space by keeping music, books, an ideas notebook, anything that inspires you, to hand. When you feel in need of a little creative help, pick up a book or play some music to get back into your creative flow. I'd recommend setting aside a couple of minutes to do this every day, as it feeds your mind and will help you face the rest of your day refreshed.

- Think about where you have your best ideas. It may be that you don't feel as creative at your desk as you do at your kitchen table or in a café.
- What would happen if you spent more time in this place?
- How can you recreate this to make sure it happens more often?
- Do you work better with a colleague than you do on your own?
- Remember a time when you've come up with an idea you've been pleased with. Were you alone or with company?

■ Make sure your toolkit of inspiring books, music and pictures is within easy reach.

4 Break the rules

The way we behave is governed by our view of the world. Years of experience mean we build up our own set of rules that we apply to whatever situation we're in. This has a nasty habit of restricting us and is a surefire way of keeping creativity locked in. A great way to stop this is to break the rules.

Let's say you're looking for ways to improve the productivity of your business. Your rules might be:

1 We use the telephone.
2 We work through our lunch hour.
3 We work on one client file before beginning another.

What happens when you break the rules?

1 We use alternative methods of speaking to customers than the telephone.
2 We all go and get some fresh air and walk round the block at lunch time.
3 We work with a wide range of clients at any one time, which is more stimulating for staff.

- Start by making a list of all the rules you have around your challenge.
- Work through them – and break every rule.
- Don't worry if it feels strange or you end up with something that you don't think is possible. The point of the exercise is to generate lots of ideas.
- Suspend judgement!

5 Go speed dating

This is a fun way to get lots of ideas quickly. Either enlist people from your own company or invite associates or family and friends to help. Set up the room with chairs in pairs. Tell everyone to find a partner, then give each pair your challenge, or different challenges if you have more than one, and ask them to brainstorm ways of solving it. They have five minutes to come up with three ideas for your problem. The pairs then sell their ideas back to the group who give their gut response and mark each one out of 10.

Allow for a bit of a breather between ideas so that each team can regroup and formulate their thoughts before selling them back to the group.

6 Use job interviews to inspire you with new ideas

Companies often spend a huge amount of time and money on interviewing candidates, the vast majority of whom will never make it through the door a second time. There are various reasons for this – poor vetting in the selection process, say, or a lack of clarity over what the job involves; perhaps a general need to test the market and discover what talent is out there. But the end result is the same – a lot of investment for little return.

Why not look at interviews as ways of gleaning different information? For example, candidates who are working with your competitors will have ideas on how to do things differently. New graduates will have a completely fresh approach and be able to offer you a very objective view of your area. They'll also be up to speed on new thinking and they'll also usually apply for a variety of jobs. In doing their pre-interview research, they will have gleaned a decent understanding of a wide variety of organisations and be privy to information or rumours that they will have picked up during interviews.

This is not meant to be a spying exercise, but it's a way of making the most of the people you're interviewing and ensuring that it doesn't turn into a waste of time.

- Think in advance about what type of information could be of benefit to your company.
- Ask candidates what is the most interesting work going on at companies where they have worked or been interviewed.
- Interview some candidates who you may feel you don't have much in common with.
- Take time to note down what you've learned and how you might best put it to use in your organisation.

7 Learn from parallel industries

We often look to our competitors for ideas on ways to improve our business. What are they doing that we could do? How can we adopt some of their successful practices in our work? Often our competitors are using techniques we might have been using ourselves a year ago and it does no harm to remember and reapply some old techniques. Remember that to be creative, you don't have to be original. Creating something 'new' can be about changing the context of an existing idea.

There's also much to be gained from looking outside our direct frame of reference. For example, when one manufacturer of a well-known toilet cleaner was looking for ways to improve the product, the required end result was a loo that was shiny and white. Rather than look at what other manufacturers were doing, they widened their parameters and asked, what else do we want to be shiny and white? The answer was teeth, so they looked at the dental care market and how products were improved and promoted within this market. They also looked at swimming pools to discover what techniques were used to produce the same outcome. In the personal care market, makers of roll-on deodorants looked to the pen market for inspiration and pinched the idea from roller ball pens.

- Look outside your current market and decide in what other areas people might be looking to achieve similar results to you.
- Meet with and question relevant people within these organisations – you're much more likely to get a favourable response than if you were trying to get similar information from your competitors.
- Creative ideas don't have to be original – there's nothing wrong with rediscovering old techniques that worked well and applying them to your current situation.

8. Create a senses box

In advance, take a trip to the supermarket and look for products that appeal to the different senses. Think loose leaf tea, rich aromatic coffee, strong flavours, textures, bright packaging. Gather them together in your senses box.

Find yourself a relaxing space and taking each of the senses in turn focus on just one at a time. Think about your challenge using firstly just sight, then sound, taste, touch and smell.

Focus on each sense to come up with new ideas or ways of looking at your challenge – write down any words or thoughts that spring to mind. Then using a simple Mind Map, relate them back to your problem.

> Gather some grass or samples of fabric to enrich the experience. You can also download some inspirational music onto an MP3 player and use this as an additional sensory experience.

9 Phone a friend

If you're stuck on a problem, it's always useful to get a new perspective. Think of someone who's good at getting things done, a trusted friend or colleague, family member or partner, and tell them about your challenge.

If that's not an option and you can't get hold of them easily, ask yourself what advice they'd give you. How would they react? What's the first thing they'd do?

10 Imagine a corporate take-over

I've heard through my excellent grapevine that Richard Branson has decided he wants a piece of the action and intends to bid for your company. Using innovative approaches, he has big plans! If you were Branson, how would you run the operation? How would you best serve your customers? Gain a greater share of the market? How does he think? How would your staff respond?

Try this exercise with any company you like and respect. To help with this, go online and print off a few pictures of your chosen company in action to get a feel for what they are about.

- Make a list of companies that inspire you. Think Apple, Innocent, IKEA and Disney.
- Go for companies that aren't direct competitors. It will help free your thinking and take you to different places.
- Use your stimuli to get inside the thinking behind this business and write down how they would

handle your challenge – what would they
do differently?

- Go with your instincts. This isn't the time to
rewrite your business plan – it's simply about
generating fast ideas.

7 LEADING CREATIVITY

Challenge: Bring a juggler into the office or ask for a volunteer among the ranks to give you all a quick lesson in juggling skills. Having new experiences is fun and will raise energy levels as well as people's productivity.

When it comes to leading and championing creativity in your business, the impetus has to come from you as the owner or manager. Your team won't suddenly start behaving differently unless you do first. So take a good look in the mirror before you begin. What signals are you sending out? What can you do to lead the way? Do you want to bring a couple of external people into your meetings to get a fresh perspective? Would it help to post some inspirational quotes or articles you've read in the loos or communal areas? There are lots of ways to kick-start this process, so pick one that you feel comfortable with and get going.

One of the biggest challenges for any small business is freeing up some time and space to allow creativity to flourish. When there are deadlines to meet, customers and shareholders to be kept happy, there's often not a lot of room left for manoeuvre. I'd encourage you to think of this not as a massive change programme, but as small steps to get you to where you want to be.

In order for you to succeed with this, you need to have some support in place to help if you come across a stumbling block. For ideas on ways to overcome these blocks, please see Chapter 8. But as a starting point, one of the best things you can do is surround yourself with happy, positive people who are willing to experiment, go with the flow and try new ideas. What's your recruitment policy at the moment? Is a positive, 'can do' attitude on the list?

For example, under its former Director-General, Greg Dyke, the BBC introduced a policy of recruiting on attitude rather than ability alone. It was thought at the time – and I as far as I know, still is – that while skills can be taught, the right attitude is something you either have or you don't. Happy people are more prepared to take risks, they can have lively debate without getting personal and are widely regarded as more creative. Constructive debate over ideas will lead to more and better ideas than if a group all signs up to the same ideas without discussion. A group of positive people will build on each others' suggestions and come to bigger ideas without anyone feeling as if they're under attack. If you can encourage your team to disagree without rancour, they'll become more creative and more effective. But building this kind of environment where creativity is welcome and encouraged means putting in place some processes that allow creative thinking to flow.

Freedom

When people feel challenged, motivated and supported, they're more likely to be creative. Excessive monitoring of progress is demotivating and will curb any spark of anything, let alone creativity. When it comes to managing and leading creativity in your business, set clear goals and then take a back seat. John Klee at 3M says, 'If you're only going to go for sure fire winners you're not going to come up with much. Ours is a culture where irreverence is encouraged – it's not about just doing what you're told to do. There's no hierarchy of ideas – great ideas can come from anyone, anywhere. You have to empower people to do the job and trust them to do the right thing.' And it seems to work. The average length of service for 3M employees in the UK and Ireland is 15 years. According to John Klee, 'People don't stay in one department in the business, they are encouraged to move around and learn new skills to ensure people are constantly learning and staying fresh.'

It's not possible to do a job effectively with someone else watching your every move. By giving your people the freedom to find their own way and come up with their own processes, you'll reap the rewards of a more motivated, more successful and more creative team.

Feedback

Positive feedback and praise are essential components of a happy and creative work environment. Don't go down the 'tough love' route. One manager I worked with shuddered at the idea of praising the people in his team. He was convinced it would backfire and they'd sit back and rest on their laurels. Yet when I asked him if he'd ever been praised, he said yes. He remembered enthusiastically his own boss giving great feedback and described feeling elated and more eager than ever to deliver the goods.

It's impossible to overestimate the importance of praise. If you're running your own business, it could be many years since anyone has told you that you're doing a great job, so it can be all too easy to forget how crucial it is. Put yourself in that manager's shoes and remember a time when you were given positive feedback. How did it feel? How did you respond?

Look outside

Encourage your staff to look outside their immediate surroundings and your industry for new ideas. What trends or changes in technology are happening that you could learn from? The broadcasting company ITV has set up a whole department called 'Imagine', with the purpose of bringing new ideas into the organisation and an injection of creativity across the business. Head of creative development, Pamela Hamilton says, 'We don't talk about it, we do it. It's about constantly upping our game, whether it's how we present something using pictures rather than words or looking to the future and forecasting trends, we always do the unexpected.'

Everyone in the team chooses an area that they're interested in, whether it be food, travel, fashion or science and technology. They then have a two-hour session every week where everyone takes it in turns to inspire each other. Pamela believes the secret to being creative is finding the time to have out-of-work experiences in work time. 'Everyone has a camera and we use it like a notebook. We look for emerging stuff. We're constantly listening, learning and thinking outside the office. It's using knowledge as currency. If you want to come up with better ideas you have to be better informed than everyone else. You need to be the first person who's seen it, to have experienced it first-hand. That feels very different to reading about it in a book.'

Google allows staff time to think and have new experiences in work time every week. What can you learn from them and the ITV Imagine team? Can you allow your people some time every week to have experiences or creative time that they then share with the rest of the team? What ideas can you borrow from ITV that would work for you?

Incentivise

If you're serious about embedding a creative approach, you need to start thinking about how you can really make sure this isn't a flash in the pan. Make creativity part of everyone's performance review. Ask each member of the team to come up with suggestions that will increase creativity in the business over the coming year and then ask them to choose one idea that they must put into action.

Inject some fun

Don't be afraid to shake things up a bit. An environment where the routine is regularly broken and unexpected things happen creates a more stimulating, energising place for everyone. It's all too easy when you've been working in the same way with the same people for a while for things to feel a bit tired. Having some fun shakes you out of this and will energise people and really encourage them genuinely to want to be there. That's a pretty good starting point for leading creativity in your business – create some space to have fun. Remember though that every company is different and what works in one company won't necessarily hit the right note in another.

In his book *Managing to Have Fun* (Pocket Books, 1997), the psychologist and management consultant Matt Weinstein says there are four principles at play when it comes to having fun at work.

1 Know your team

Who are the people in your team? What kinds of things do they enjoy? What do they do to relax when they're not at work? How can you tally the way they have fun with the way they are rewarded at work? The more you know the people who work with you, the more successful you will be at getting it right and motivating them.

There is an excellent example of this in *Managing to Have Fun*. A secretary called Sarah Fizer who had been in the same job for years and hated it for most of that time describes how her work life completely changed with the arrival of a new boss. One day he came to her desk at 9am and gave her a 35-page document and asked for it to be typed up, corrected and ready by 10.30. As she worked through it, she came to page 10 and found a Post-it™ Note. 'If you get this back to me in less than an hour, I will take you out for lunch on Thursday.' On page 17 she found a miniature chocolate taped to the page with another note: 'You're almost half way through – eat this immediately!'

Little Post-it™ Notes are now part of every day life for Sarah, but she says, 'Do you know what made that first time feel really special? I knew that while he was composing his report he was thinking about me, about my having to type it up for him. And he thought about how to make that fun for me. That he would think about me making my way through that long report when I wasn't even around – that was totally different from anything that's ever happened around here before.'

2 Set an example

People look to their managers to set the tone on how to act. If the boss doesn't let go a bit, the staff won't either. No one wants to be out of step with management so people aren't going to relax enough to be more creative if this isn't what's going on at the top. You can't ask someone to do something you wouldn't be prepared to do yourself. This might involve you going out on a limb.

For example, Paul Hidden, a senior manager with LloydsTSB, wanted to change the culture in his part of the business. 'It was at a time when having a radio on or not wearing a suit to work was considered radical. I think my guys thought I was bit mad at first when I had a sign on my desk that read "choose your attitude". I explained that we all choose what mood we are in and we can choose to look at things in a positive way if we want to.

'The difference in perception on hearing "I'll do all that I can" as opposed to "I'll do what I can" is enormous. What this led to was improved business relationships, higher customer satisfaction scores (people were inclined to be more generous, even if things hadn't gone 100%, because they thought you'd tried) and a genuine improvement in productivity levels. People actually liked coming to work because relationships were good and they didn't dread the phone ringing!'

Last Christmas, the management at Clear wanted to recognise everyone's hard work and commitment over the year. It had been a particularly busy 12 months and people had worked long hours to meet deadlines. So on the last working day before Christmas, one of the directors, dressed in full Santa Claus gear, came in carrying a huge sack of presents – one for every employee. They had been chosen with care. For example, a support team member who was going on a trip over Christmas received a digital camera – a great choice. There was dinner for two at a nice restaurant for an employee who had spent a lot of time travelling with work and didn't get to spend much time with her partner. You get the picture.

But what was more important than the gifts was the fun and sense of occasion when he walked through the door in his red suit and white beard. Everyone loved it and shared in the fun. When he came back to his desk in his normal clothes someone joked, 'Oh Steven, you should have been here five minutes ago. You just missed Father Christmas!'

3 This is about you as well as your team

Having fun at work is not just for the benefit of your employees – it's about you too. It's very easy to feel disconnected and a bit isolated at the top, but if you can find ways to engage on an emotional basis with your team, you will also reap the rewards. Melvin Jay, founding director of Clear says: 'Make sure you feel how people are feeling and don't let small things get blown up into big things. It's important to always try to head off an issue at the pass, as it's amazing how quickly an issue can snowball if it's ignored. Listen, empathise, be fair, but don't be a push-over.'

After a team away-day, a former boss of mine made the comment, 'when we take time out to spend some time together, we remember we actually like each other'. It's sad that these occasions seem to be rare events. When you're stuck in to the fast pace of work, it's hard to look up and enjoy the company of your colleagues. As the boss, when you have some fun with your staff, even for two minutes to share a joke, it changes the atmosphere and people feel different, more upbeat and confident.

4 It won't happen overnight

If you want to change the culture in your business, realise that you won't do it overnight. Be patient: this process is about small steps, not one huge leap. If the atmosphere in your office is generally pretty staid and sombre, it's not going to suddenly become fun-loving and creative at a single stroke.

Start by introducing small changes that recognise achievement and celebrate success. Paul Hidden (LloydsTSB) says, 'I always believed that people would take a while to respond in a creative fashion – after all we'd just spent a decade "beating the creativity out of them". But in instigating some small changes, we'd made a start and just needed to build on these by giving people permission to have a bit of fun whilst getting the job done. As ever when trying to get things changed, communication was the key. Explaining that there was a business rationale behind the changes – in other words, that there was "something in it for the bank" – somehow made the staff more accepting of the change.'

He then introduced a series of measures designed to get his team thinking and acting creatively. One of them was setting up 'Ideas Friday' where the team stopped work for an hour and brainstormed the problems and challenges that had happened during the week. It was carried out in teams and the team that generated the most ideas, not necessarily the best, chose what non-work activity they'd do together that evening.

'As a result of the idea generation, lots of little things got changed but it made the team feel involved and that they were in control of the environment. So if we hit unexpected problems, say an unforecast rise in volumes, then they were always happy to suggest solutions.'

Teresa Amabile, professor of business administration at Harvard Business School, has conducted a great deal of research into this subject and says people are most creative when they are primarily motivated by interest, enjoyment, satisfaction and the challenge of work itself. She says managers should focus on these key areas if they want to lead a creative movement in their business.

1 Challenging work

People work best when they feel challenged, are excited by their work and feel they are learning. A certain amount of pressure can be regarded as positive if it's in the context of, say, an intellectually challenging piece of work. This is distinct from excessive workload pressure which has a negative effect on creativity. Try to give your team work that is stimulating and plays to their strengths.

2 Freedom

Individuals are more creative when they feel they have control over their day-to-day tasks. Set clear goals and then let your people get on with it. You've employed them to do a job and they will do it better if they're not being constantly monitored – let them come up with their own ways of solving the challenges they face.

3 Resources

Ensure you have adequate resources to support the project. Creativity requires an investment of both time and funding, so it's worth making certain you apportion both appropriately. People are also affected psychologically by how a project is resourced – it gives them an indication as to how the project is valued within the organisation.

4 Work group encouragement

When choosing your team – be it your entire staff or a team for a specific project – variety is key when you want to encourage creativity, as it exposes everyone to different attitudes and new approaches. Look for individuals who have different perspectives and opinions but who value each other and the work involved.

5 Organisational encouragement

As a manager, ensuring individuals feel supported and valued is part of your role, but it's vital when it comes to creating the right environment for creativity. 'Permission to fail' may now feel like a bit of a cliché but the sentiment is as relevant as ever. It's important they know they won't be out of a job if they do something different and it doesn't go to plan. Try to engage the whole business in what you want to achieve. While it's great for individuals and teams to have the support of the boss, there's no replacement for the whole organisation being behind your idea. It means the initiative takes on a life of its own which is of enormous value to those involved.

(Amabile, T M, Conti, R, Coon, H, Lazenby, J and Herron, M, 'Assessing the work environment for creativity,' *Academy of Management Journal*)

Think about the messages you are sending out to your staff. Only by making it a top-down, inside-out process will creativity become a way of life. Whatever your business, with the right leadership it can and will become more creative.

Exercise

With your journal to hand, consider the following questions and jot down your thoughts.

- How do you encourage new ideas and suggestions in the team?
- How do you react when individuals come up with suggestions?
- What does this tell you about yourself?
- How can you make your work or meetings more fun?
- What action do you generally take as a result of ideas or suggestions from the team?
- Are people generally up for new ways of working?
- How are people rewarded for coming up with ideas?
- Do people feel free to tell it how it is without fear of the consequences?
- Think of a challenge you are currently facing. How might you tackle this creatively?

8 MAKING IT HAPPEN

Challenge: Once a week, arrange for your team to come together over lunch or coffee and take it in turns to inspire each other with the creative work going on in your business. Share tips from successful projects, interesting articles or books you've read. It will broaden everyone's knowledge and help you all stay fresh.

'Anyone who has ever taken a shower has had an idea. It's the person who gets out of the shower, dries off and does something about it who makes the difference.' Nolan Bushell, founder of Atari

It's all very well talking about being more creative, but doing something about it is what counts. You can have hundreds of ideas but if you don't do anything with them, it's a waste of time and energy.

Companies are very fond of initiatives: let's hold regular social gatherings or let's bring in a guest speaker once a month, and so on – the latest thing designed to rally the troops and inspire action. I'm not knocking these ideas; more often than not, they come from a genuine desire to improve everyone's working life, but all too often before you know it, a few months have passed, nothing has happened and the flavour of the month has changed. Don't let this happen with creativity in your business. Not just because it's disheartening and demoralising for your team to see something that they get behind and feel excited about bite the dust. But also because it's far too important to your bottom line to let slip.

Generally speaking, the bigger companies grow, the less creative they become. As a business expands, it often becomes more focused on its core offering: the product or service that has led to its success. This in turn leaves less room for new offers, which carry an inherent risk – they may be successful, but no one can guarantee it – and can lead to a reduction in creativity. Larger organisations require more processes to operate smoothly. If there are half a dozen of you in an office, everyone knows what everyone else is doing without the need for formalities. This natural flow of information and knowledge doesn't happen in larger businesses, which inevitably leads to the introduction of official procedures which again get in the way of creativity. As you're running a small business, take heart: chances are that you're already way more creative than your bigger competitors. Small companies are nimble and open to all sorts of possibilities. The answer to the question 'Can we do this?' is generally 'Yes!'

Turning a bunch of great ideas into a successful initiative and then making sure that regular idea generation becomes a permanent part of your business's life isn't always plain sailing. It's worth thinking about where you are with this. What journey are you on? Where do you want to get to? If you acknowledge upfront that there will be obstacles along the way and are prepared to deal with them, it will make your journey a smoother one. You'll recognise them if they do arise, and will know how to respond.

Potential barriers

Fear of failure

No-one wants to fail, but if yours is an environment where some ideas are seen as right and others wrong, it will inhibit – if not stamp out – creativity. People have to be allowed to take risks and make mistakes. How many times have you read about a famous pop star, author or entrepreneur who was turned down many times before signing the deal that made them rich? Take J K Rowling. Her Harry Potter books were rejected by numerous publishers before she was discovered by Bloomsbury. Walt Disney was turned down by hundreds of banks before he secured the money for Disneyworld. You'd imagine he might have given up after a hundred rejections, but no!

Failure and making mistakes is a healthy (if initially painful) part of life and that includes work. It's to be encouraged. Some organisations even reward mistakes. I don't think you need to go this far – it could be a costly business! – but by letting everyone know that getting knocked back happens to everyone and is part and parcel of life, it will send a message that they have permission to try something different.

'We've been here before' syndrome

If your business is well established or you've had considerable experience of working in another industry before starting up your company, it's easy to get into the habit of writing off ideas before someone has even finished presenting them. People have long memories and often enjoy telling 'war stories' of how such and such didn't work in the past, so won't work now. If you find yourself judging ideas at the earliest stage, you need to nip this in the bud! Your negativity has a profound impact not only on creativity but on the people around you. Ideas need time to grow and cutting them off before they've reached their prime is not only unhelpful, but will kill creativity in its tracks.

No idea is a bad idea

You need to generate lots of ideas before you can come up with one that 'sticks'. That doesn't mean that the others are a waste of time; they're all part of the innovation process. Sometimes the most obvious ideas are dismissed because they threaten the status quo or challenge long-held, never-questioned values. Bottled water is a good example. It was launched at a time when drinking water was considered to be a commodity that should be freely available to all. However, what originally seemed like a commercial non-starter has turned into a major sector of the soft drinks market. Always ask yourself: on what basis am I rejecting this idea? It might be the next bottled water!

Don't assume you know who the creative people are in your business

Look around your company; is it always the same people who seem to come up with ideas? It's a common assumption that some people are more creative than others, yet there are countless examples in businesses where it's not the most obvious person who's come up with the big idea. At 3M, it was someone in sales who discovered the tape that could peel off which resulted in the creation of Scotch Tape™. It's important to find a way to encourage everyone to contribute to the creative process. For instance, have a suggestion box where all staff can input their suggestions and highlight the contents at regular staff meetings.

Overcoming barriers

Awareness is the key to overcoming any potential 'roadblocks'. If you know what they are and recognise them when you see them ahead, you'll stand a much better chance of being able to take the right action when it happens.

Hone your listening skills

Active listening is a great skill and one to be encouraged in every organisation whatever its size. It's about helping individuals better understand their situation, their experiences and their feelings without judging them or jumping to conclusions. It involves helping them work out their own solutions to challenges rather than telling them the answer. A useful way to do this is to ask questions to clarify understanding and paraphrase what the other person has said to check you haven't misinterpreted what they've said.

As a manager or team leader, listening can be about listening for what's unsaid as well as what's said – as a colleague of mine puts it, listening to the silences. And it's also about showing that you're listening in what you say and by non-verbal clues, like maintaining eye contact and showing you are interested and focused on the speaker.

Notice your own reaction to the conversation. Ask yourself

why you might be feeling like this. If you find yourself reacting negatively, question your motives for this. What would make you feel positive? Is this about you or the other person?

Recognise creativity

Voicing an idea can feel like a risky business. If you want to encourage people to speak up when they have a spark of an idea, then they need to know it's going to be recognised. There are many ways to encourage people to come up with ideas, e.g. ideas boards in a communal area like beside a photocopier, or formal ideas meetings. It's really important, though, to follow up on ideas and keep everyone informed about what's happening. It may be that it's not possible to action a particular idea, but you're planning to do something else along similar lines. Let everyone know – if people feel their ideas have been ignored, they're less likely to contribute in the future.

Understand the power of diversity

Different people will bring different skills to the melting pot. In fact, those who come up with the ideas may not always be the best ones to put them into practice. The real value of working in a team comes from different individuals who have a range of skills working together to make things happen in your organisation. Not everyone will work in the same way. Some are good at coming up with ideas on the spot, others have a more reflective style and will want to go away and think before voicing their ideas. Make sure you allow for all styles of thinking in your business.

Road-test your ideas

At some stage, it's time to take a break from idea generation and move on to idea analysis, so that you can work out which make the grade and may have a practical application to your company, and which don't. Think back to why you wanted something new and assess ideas against their ability to deliver. Were you hoping to increase sales or bring in new customers, for example?

Create a scoring system mixed with a healthy dose of 'gut feel' and see how your ideas measure up. It's important to amend your ideas in the light of your evaluation. Maybe the price needs to change to better reflect what customers will pay? Or do you need to introduce a more economical form of packaging?

Allow some flex

When it comes to assessing your ideas, there'll be some that you must have and other areas where you can compromise. It's worth having a think upfront about what these areas might be. It may be that you have to be flexible about some of the nice-to-haves, but want to stick to your guns on others. This can change as you go along but it will make the journey less painful if you've considered some of the possibilities in advance.

Set some goals

If you go on a course or pick up a book on a subject you're interested in, you'll no doubt find yourself hearing or reading about the importance of setting goals. So it is here! You're much more likely to succeed with a plan if you've written it down. So in your notebook, commit to setting some goals. Earl Nightingale was an American self-development expert and author. He came to the conclusion that 'we become what we think about' – if he's right, it highlights the importance of setting goals. It keeps your mind on the job and focuses thinking.

A good place to start is actually at the end. Close your eyes and think about where you want to be in six months' time. What will people say about your organisation then? How will your staff or team feel? What does success look like? How will you feel? How will it be different to now? Take a few deep breaths and take time to really enjoy this feeling.

Involve others

Embarking on any kind of change can sometimes leave you feeling isolated. It's important to surround yourself with people who you know will support and encourage you. Identify who these key people are and draw yourself a 'people map'.

Find a large piece of paper and write down who your supporters and challengers might be. Why do you think this?

What can you do to make your supporters louder and your challengers quieter?

Keep up your momentum

This is a journey and it's important that you keep up your momentum and drive. What's going to keep you going? Who's going to support you, both at work and away from the office? How are you going to secure that support? What are you going to do to reward yourself? Whether you decide to take yourself out for a coffee with a book you've wanted to read for ages or buy a new gadget, make sure you celebrate your little successes along the way. It will help sustain you and make it a more pleasant ride!

Know when you arrive

It's all very well having a plan, but how will you know when you've arrived at your destination? It's important that you recognise the view when you get there. Paint a picture of what success will look like. Who is in this picture? What are they doing? What conversations are they having? And again, reward yourself and your team when you've made it. At Clear, the directors celebrated winning their first big contract by buying a nice coffee machine for everyone in the office to enjoy. It was a tangible way to celebrate all the hard work that had been put in to winning the project and gave out a signal that success was something to be enjoyed by the whole team.

Make sure you know when you arrive. That's not to say there's an end point to creativity, that you stop when you get there. But it's important to enjoy your success and take some time out to really drink in all that you've achieved. Creativity is, of course, a living, breathing thing that evolves and changes and you and your team will want to change and move with it.

It might be interesting and even amusing to look back at your journal and to the comments you jotted down at the beginning of this book. You've travelled on a journey during the course of the book and are now at a different place than when you began. How do you like your new surroundings? Are you feeling any different?

My hope is that you believe deep down that you are indeed a creative mastermind with far more ideas than you ever thought possible – and that you believe the same of your colleagues. We all shine more brightly when we believe in ourselves and know that others believe in *us*.

This book isn't intended as a set of rules that you follow rigidly. It's food for thought and works best when you take what you want from it and add to it your own ingredients, seasoning and colour.

I wish you lots of luck on your adventure and happy creating!

INDEX